HOW TO WIN AT THE
Casino

BELINDA LEVEZ

First published in 2004 by New Holland (Publishers) Ltd
London • Cape Town • Sydney • Auckland
www.newhollandpublishers.com

Garfield House	80 McKenzie St	14 Aquatic Drive	218 Lake Rd
86 Edgware Rd	Cape Town	Frenchs Forest	Northcote
London W2 2EA	8001	NSW 2086	Auckland
United Kingdom	South Africa	Australia	New Zealand

Publisher: Mariëlle Renssen

Publishing managers: Claudia Dos Santos/Simon Pooley

Designer: Sheryl Buckley

Editor: Katja Splettstoesser

Illustrations: Anton Krügel

Picture researchers: Sonya Meyer, Karla Kik

Production: Myrna Collins

Proofreader: Gill Gordon

ISBN 1 84330 770 7

Reproduction by Hirt & Carter (Cape) Pty Ltd

Printed and bound in Singapore by Kyodo Printing Co Pte Ltd

10 9 8 7 6 5 4

contents

The Casino Experience

A casino embodies the concept of a luxurious, glamorous and timeless environment, which has its own language, currency and etiquette. Casinos provide the location and facilities for players to try their luck at a wide range of gambling games, in which the casino acts as banker, paying out winning bets and collecting losing bets. Working under strict controls aimed at preventing cheating, professional dealers called croupiers operate the games, which include roulette, blackjack, punto banco, poker, craps and slot machines. In general, casinos can be divided into two categories. City-centre casinos tend to be more formal, imposing stricter dress codes and relatively high minimum stakes. Resort and smaller provincial casinos, which are usually more relaxed, allow casual wear and offer lower minimum stakes.

and shouting and constant commentary from the stickman. The card tables tend to be more sedate, with players concentrating on the hands they have been dealt.

Away from the hustle and bustle of the gaming halls, most casinos have private rooms (called *salons privés*) to cater for the high-staking players who prefer to bet in a secluded environment.

Resort casinos, and most US casinos, are usually part of large leisure complexes that include hotels, restaurants and a range of entertainment and sports facilities. The gaming floors are often huge, with row upon row of slot machines, including linked machines promising huge jackpot payouts.

They have separate rooms or areas for keno (which is played in a theatre-like arena), and baccarat, which attracts big spenders. Most casinos in Europe tend to be small intimate club-style establishments, and are often located in or near the centre of the city.

The first area encountered on a visit to a casino is the lobby or entrance hall. Here reception personnel provide information and assistance to visitors and deal with any membership formalities. At some casinos, car jockeys (valets) take care of parking, while at others, parking lots may be located some way from the complex.

THE PHYSICAL ENVIRONMENT

Casinos are often busy, noisy places. In European casinos, the quieter games, such as roulette and blackjack, are the most popular; while in the USA, slot machines and craps are favoured. In roulette, frenzied betting is interspersed with calm as players watch the wheel to see the winning number. By contrast the craps tables are the noisiest in the casino, with players cheering

TOP *Recalling the golden era of Hollywood, the lavish MGM Grand in Las Vegas incorporates 16 restaurants, the Showbar Lounge, the Forever Grand Wedding Chapel and Grand Garden Arena.*

Electronic items like mobile phones, computers, calculators and radios are not allowed on the gaming floor. Taking photographs is also not permitted.

To reach the gaming tables, players generally have to pass through the noisy, vibrant slot machine area. Slots are easy to play, and most stakes are low, so the slot halls are usually crowded. Flashing lights, bells and sirens, and the clatter of coins being paid out all add to the excitement. All types of mechanical and electronic games, from the old-fashioned one-armed bandits to video poker, can be played, and interactive video games are increasingly available.

The main gaming halls are lavishly decorated, often to a theme, but the focal points are the green or blue baize-covered tables printed with betting layouts. Seating for players is provided around the tables, which are arranged in groups, called pits.

A croupier (dealer) runs the game at each table, and groups of tables are watched over by inspectors. Pens and paper are supplied for players to note the numbers spun on roulette, although nowadays, electronic signs at each roulette table indicate the last numbers spun.

Casinos in the USA often incorporate bookmakers. Called the race and sports book, the 'bookies' take bets on horse racing, greyhound racing and sporting events from around the world, satellite broadcasts of which are shown on huge screens.

RIGHT *A new way to 'break the bank'? Casinos make it increasingly easy for players to win more money with less effort – even going so far as to place cash machines right on the gaming floor.*

Cash point

At the cash point (the cage), in the main gaming area, a variety of financial transactions are carried out, such as cashing cheques (checks), applying for credit, exchanging money for chips and cashing in winnings. Players can use local or foreign currency, or traveller's cheques to purchase chips. Some casinos even accept foreign currencies at the gaming tables, but credit cards are not always readily accepted and the amounts that can be cashed on them are limited. Where casinos are lenient with credit betting, applications can be made at the cash point, or in advance by phone, post or e-mail. Most casinos now have ATMs (automatic teller machines) located near the cash point.

Private rooms

Private rooms, called *salons privés* in Europe, are found mostly in the higher staking casinos and are reserved for medium- to high-staking players, allowing them to bet in a more secluded environment away from spectators. Private rooms, which are staffed by the casino's most experienced dealers, contain tables for games like roulette, blackjack and baccarat. Favoured customers, the really high rollers, are often afforded the privacy of a totally private room for their exclusive use.

Membership requirements

In some countries, casinos require players to become members before they will admit them. Applications for membership must be made either in person or in writing, depending on the casino's rules. The straightforward procedure requires that prospective members give personal details such as name and address, and a declaration that they are old enough to gamble.

The minimum age for gambling is usually the age of majority, commonly 18 years. In the USA players must be over 21, and in Switzerland over 20. Identification, such as a passport or driver's licence, may be asked for.

Membership is a legal requirement for entry into most UK casinos. Players must apply 24 hours beforehand and must provide identification. Casinos reserve the right to refuse membership applications. A player who is barred from one casino may find it difficult to obtain membership for another, as the names of barred members are often circulated to other casinos within a group or in the same area.

BELOW *The salon privé, or private room, is for high rollers: gamblers who are willing to play for higher minimum stakes than those in the main gaming hall.*

Casino personnel

▶ Casino personnel wear uniforms to identify their position easily. These are often a variation on evening wear, with the men wearing bow ties and waistcoats, and the women in long dresses. The inspectors, pit bosses and managers are dressed in formal suits or tuxedos. General managers usually wear business (dress) suits. In resort casinos, which often have a strong décor theme, uniforms tend to be less formal and reflect the overall design concept.

▶ Each table is operated by at least one dealer (croupier), who is responsible for running the game and operating the equipment. On card tables (blackjack and poker), this includes shuffling and dealing the cards. On roulette, the dealer spins the ball. The dealer's duties vary with each game, but include changing money into chips, placing players' bets, giving instructions about the game, paying out winning bets and collecting losing bets on the casino's behalf, and monitoring players' behaviour.

▶ Inspectors watch over the tables. They are responsible for checking that the dealer is operating the game correctly and that players are neither cheating nor being cheated. Each inspector may monitor more than one table. He or she checks large payouts and keeps records of how much each

TOP RIGHT *Dealers are always friendly, well-groomed and dressed stylishly.*

Dress code

Casinos reserve the right to refuse entrance to players who do not meet required dress codes. Casinos may have different standards for daytime and evening gaming, with more relaxed rules during the day. Upmarket casinos, especially those that require membership, insist that players are smartly dressed, with men expected to wear a jacket and tie. Resort casinos generally allow casual wear at all times, but the rules for individual establishments can vary considerably, so it is best to confirm what the requirements are before setting out. Jeans, T-shirts, beach wear, sports attire and manual work clothes are often not allowed.

player spends and wins. The inspector notes how many high denomination chips are given to a player, and resolves any disputes that may arise between dealers and players.

If a problem occurs, such as a player not agreeing with the amount the dealer has paid out for a winning bet, or a winning chip being cleared away in error, the dealer will summon the inspector by making a kissing noise. This particular sound is used as it is easily heard through the noise of a casino hall. As all table games are recorded on videotape, any disputes like these are quickly and easily resolved.

▶ Each group of tables is meticulously controlled by a pit boss, who is responsible for allocating staff to the respective tables and for carefully checking the work of the dealers and the inspectors. The pit boss collates particular information about how much an individual player is spending and passes this on to the managers. He or she also collates details about how much money a specific player is winning. This information is subsequently relayed to the cash point so when the player cashes in at the end of a gaming session, the cashier is assured that the chips have been legitimately won, and were not acquired by cheating or pickpocketing.

RIGHT *In the security control room, trained personnel constantly monitor the action at the tables and on the gaming floor, looking for any evidence of cheating.*

▶ Casino managers deal with the day to day running of the casino. They socialize with players and allocate complimentary benefits such as drinks, meal vouchers, cigarettes, hotel rooms or show tickets.

A player's level of spending determines what complimentary benefits he or she receives, with the highest staking customers sometimes receiving everything free. Regular slot machine players can join a special club which allows them to accumulate points that count towards these benefits.

▶ Casinos keep records of how much individuals win or lose. In countries where casinos are state controlled, the records may be scrutinized by government agencies who may request details of players who regularly spend large amounts of money.

▶ Security staff constantly mingle with players. Some are uniformed, while others are plain-clothed. Casinos use a variety of electronic surveillance systems to monitor the action on the gaming floors. All games are recorded, and the tapes are stored for a period of time, so that in the event of a dispute they can be played back.

▶ While uniformed security personnel look out for pickpockets and chip snatchers on the gaming floors, behind-the-scenes staff watch the surveillance cameras. If a player is suspected of cheating, he or she will be closely watched from the control room. Players caught cheating will be photographed before being thrown out. Casinos share information about cheats, so they can be refused entry to other casinos.

TOP *High denomination chips from Sun City, South Africa. Each casino's chips are unique and cannot be used anywhere else.*

Casino currency

⊛ Instead of playing with money, gamblers use coloured plastic or metal discs, called chips. This enables the games to run quickly and smoothly, as the chips can be piled up into stacks and easily counted. Players can purchase chips at the cash point (in any currency), or on the gaming tables (in the local currency).

⊛ Each casino has its own set of chips that can only be used in that particular establishment. However, if a casino is part of a group, it may be possible for cash chips from one location to be used at another casino in the same group.

⊛ Lower denomination chips are disc-shaped (round). Higher denomination chips, known as plaques or biscuits, are rectangular or oval.

⊛ There are two types of chips – cash chips and table chips. Cash chips are the casino's general currency. They can be used to buy into any games, place bets, pay for food and drinks and to tip the staff. Each chip is marked with the cash value, the name of the casino and the casino's logo. Cash chips are often referred to by their colour. For example, in London casinos £5 chips are called reds, £25 chips are blacks, £100 chips are pinks, and £1 chips are referred to as singles.

- On leaving the casino, all cash chips are returned to the cash point to be exchanged for money or a cheque.

- Table chips are only used for playing the game on that particular table. To buy them, place your money or cash chips on the table, making sure they are not on the betting layout, and ask the dealer for 'colour'. The dealer will give you table chips to the correspon-ding value. Before leaving, ask the dealer to exchange your table chips for cash chips. Some casinos allow players to bet by placing cash onto the betting layout. The dealer exchanges it for a marker, announcing 'money plays'. If a cash bet wins it is paid out in chips.

BELOW *When cash is exchanged for table chips, the stack is broken down to prove the correct amount is being handed over.*

CASINO ETIQUETTE

Players are expected to abide by a number of particular conventions in order to facilitate the uninterrupted running of the games. These can be summed up as follows:
- Do not engage the dealer in conversation
- Do not put money or chips into the dealer's hand
- Do not throw chips or money at the betting layout
- Never move another player's bet.

▶ Although all dealers are trained to be friendly and welcoming, they must also pay attention to the game and be alert for cheats. If you try to engage a dealer in casual conversation he or she may ignore you, as distracting dealers is a trick frequently used by cheats. If you need assistance, the best person to approach is one of the floor managers, as their duties include socializing with play-ers. If you have a query about a game, ask the dealer to call an inspector.

▶ Security requirements prevent dealers from taking anything directly from a player's hand or possessions such as handbags (purses) or jackets. Dealers are also not allowed to shake hands with players, to prevent them from covertly passing across chips.

▶ Throwing chips at the betting layout can result in other bets being knocked away from the correct place. On large tables, such as roulette and baccarat, if you cannot reach the area where you want to place a bet, simply put the chip on the table in front of you and call out loudly and clearly to the dealer where it should go. The dealer will repeat your instructions and place the bet. Unless you are actually buying chips or betting, never put money, cash chips or table chips directly onto the table or the betting layout, as it will be assumed that you are making a bet.

▶ On roulette, the first player to bet with cash chips takes precedence, and no-one else may bet with the same value cash chips. Other players will be warned that someone is betting with cash chips as the dealer will announce, for example, 'reds on' or 'pinks on' (depending on the colour of the cash chips).

▶ Do not leave your chips unattended at the tables, as it is quite likely that they will be stolen. The exception is poker, where the dealer will watch a player's chips during a leave of absence from the table.

▶ Players should not touch any gaming equipment or cards unless instructed to do so by the dealer. In some casinos, blackjack players are not allowed to touch the cards at all, while in poker, where players hold their own cards, the cards must be kept in view at all times.

▶ Never straighten up or move another player's bet. If you need to place your chips on top of someone else's chips and their bet is ambiguously placed, query the bet with the dealer before making any sudden moves.

▶ Players should wait until all the winning bets have been paid out before placing bets on the next game. The dealer will give the cue by announcing 'place your bets' when it is time for the next game to begin.

▶ Dealers are given a strict set of procedures to follow, such as paying out all winning bets in a specific order. So even though you may be in a great hurry to leave the casino, it is useless to try to convince the dealer that your bet is paid out before your turn.

Games played

Most casinos offer a wide choice of games, loosely based on the three basic items of equipment used in gaming – cards, dice and wheels. Mechanical games (those that use wheels or other moving equipment) include roulette, slots, boule, big six wheel, and a form of lottery called keno. Craps, two-up and Sic Bo are all played with dice, or tokens such as coins. Card games include blackjack, poker, punto banco (also called *chemin de fer* or baccarat) and red-dog.

The games played in casinos vary from country to country. Some games have a number of international variations which are known by different names, others are seldom played outside their country of origin. Poker, craps and slot machines are commonly found in the USA and in international resort casinos, whereas European casinos tend to have traditional games, like French roulette, boules and *chemin de fer*. Two-up is confined to Australian casinos. As the name suggests, Caribbean stud poker is particularly popular in that region.

Many casinos produce leaflets outlining the various rules and providing brief details on how to play each of the games. Some casinos also give lessons at quieter times of the day, enabling aspirant players to try the games and learn the rules without losing any money in the process.

TOP *French playing cards use different terms for the court cards, although the pictures are similar to the English language cards used in most casinos.*

Casino cards are usually larger than normal playing cards. The two standard packs (decks) of cards commonly used in casinos worldwide are the English language cards and French language cards that differ only in the symbols marked on the court (or picture) cards.

In the English pack the King, Queen and Jack are marked with the symbols K, Q and J respectively, while the French cards use R, D and V (standing for *Roi*, *Dame* and *Valet*). Although the symbols differ, the cards are easily identified by the pictures, and players using an unfamiliar deck should not be confused.

In this book, English cards have been used consistently throughout to illustrate the games.

GAMES OF CHANCE AND SKILL

Casinos offer a choice between games of skill, where the player can affect the outcome; and chance, where players have no input and rely on luck.

Games of chance include roulette, slots and punto banco. Once players have decided what numbers to play there is no further action to take.

Poker and blackjack are games of skill. As players make all the decisions about taking cards, they are able to use their intelligence and experience at the game to win. With games of skill, a combination of knowledge, common sense and savvy can make the big difference between winning and losing.

THE GAME PLAN

Stakes

Casinos impose both minimum and maximum stakes on each table game. The minimum stake is the lowest amount that can be bet on a game; the maximum is the highest amount that may be bet. However, within each game, the stake levels on different tables may vary. For example, in roulette, some tables will offer a low minimum stake (for example $5), while others have a higher minimum stake (such as $10). To enter a game, players must bet the minimum amount, but they have the option of betting up to the maximum stake; it is not mandatory. A sign on the gaming table, or suspended above it, indicates the table stakes. Each game has different stakes, and individual bets may differ within the stake level. The value of the table chips is automatically the value of the minimum stake. The lowest staking tables are often the most crowded, and the highest staking tables are located in the *salon privé*.

Bets within a game may also vary. On roulette the minimum stake on the outside bets may be higher than the minimum on the inside bets. Although the value of the table chips is the minimum stake, customers may request a higher

value. For example, the minimum stake on a roulette table may be $2 (meaning that each colour chip is worth $2). If a player requests that his or her chips are marked to, say $25, a special marker is used to denote the new value of the chips.

Casinos often have lower minimum stakes during the quieter mid-week period, increasing the stakes over weekends and holidays, when the casino is busy.

The odds

The odds tell players how much they could win for a particular stake. Odds are quoted for each type of bet in a game. Some odds are printed directly on the betting layout (for example, 'Insurance pays 2 to 1' on blackjack tables), but these are only some of the bets that can be played, each offering different odds.

A sign listing all the odds for a particular game will be on the table, hanging over it, or close by. The list gives the name of the

TOP RIGHT *This sign on the blackjack table lets players know that it is a high-staking game for advanced players.*

bet and the odds paid, allowing players to decide how they want to bet.

The odds are quoted as two numbers, like 2 to 1, or 8 to 1. The number on the left is the amount won if the number on the right is staked. For odds of 2 to 1, if one chip is staked two chips will be won and the player keeps the stake, so a total of three chips will be won. For odds of 3 to 2, if 1 chip is staked, one and a half chips will be won and the player keeps the stake. Total winnings are therefore two and a half chips. For a five-chip bet on odds of 2 to 1, five multiplies the odds so 2 to 1 becomes 10 to 5. This means that for a five-chip bet, 10 chips are won and the player keeps the stake, giving total winnings of 15 chips.

An alternative way of writing the odds is to put a slash or a colon between the two numbers, so 2 to 1 becomes 2/1 or 2:1.

Probability

If a coin is tossed, there is a 50 per cent chance that it will land on heads and a 50 per cent chance that it will land on tails. However, this does not mean that if you toss a coin 100 times it will actually land 50 times on heads and 50 times on tails. After a large number of tosses the number of heads and tails will be approximately equal, but there is no way that the outcome of one particular toss can be accurately predicted.

When betting on roulette, many players make the mistake of assuming that because a number has not been spun for a long time that it must be due on their next up-and-coming throw. Over time it will be spun again, but a player could wait all night for a specific number to eventually come up.

Evens

The odds of evens are an exception: no numbers are quoted. It is actually odds of one to one (1/1) and is often called 'even money'. The outside bets on roulette (black, red; even, odd; high, low) are often called the even chances because they pay odds of evens. A $10 bet on an even chance pays $20. ($10 is the winnings and $10 is the returned stake.)

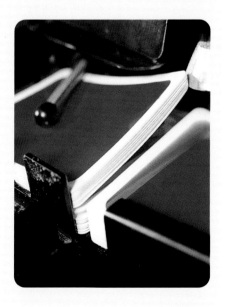

RIGHT *Shuffling machines now perform one of the dealer's tasks. They are fast, efficient, and are not subject to human error.*

House advantage

The odds paid by casinos for winning bets on most games are not the true chances of winning the game. Casinos make a profit by paying out bets at odds that are less than the true chances of winning. This difference is called the 'house advantage' or 'edge', and it is usually stated as a percentage.

The house advantage for different games varies. For some games, such as blackjack, however, an average is quoted, as the house advantage changes throughout the game.

Using roulette as an example, you can see how the house advantage works. A roulette wheel with one zero is marked with the numbers 1–36 inclusive, plus zero. This gives a possible 37 numbers that can be spun. By placing a bet on every single number, players can guarantee that they will have a win. This would cost the player 37 chips. The player will be paid odds of 35 to 1 for the winning number. That means he or she would win 36 (35+1) chips. However since it cost 37 chips the player has actually lost one chip. If a player continues in this manner eventually all his or her chips will end up with the casino, as every spin of the wheel would cost one chip.

On a roulette wheel with two zeros there are 38 numbers in total but the odds paid for a winning number remain 35 to 1. If one chip is bet on every number, the casino wins two chips on every spin of the wheel.

Comparison of House Advantage on Different Games

	%
Blackjack	5.6
Dice	from >1–16.7*
Punto Banco	up to 5
Roulette with one zero	2.7
Roulette with two zeros	5.26

(* depends on the type of bet)

BELOW *The Fremont Street Experience in Las Vegas lures gamblers to its casinos.*

Commission

On games such as dice and punto banco, the casino pays true odds on some bets, but charges a commission on the payout. This is usually a percentage of the stake, but is sometimes a percentage of the winnings.

In poker, where players bet among themselves, the casino charges either a percentage of the pot or an hourly rate. Poker is open to many ways of cheating, but by using casino facilities, players can ensure they are playing fair games.

Stake level

Your gaming budget will determine your stake level. If you start with $1000 for example, betting one chip per spin on a $10 roulette table will last 100 spins. With a spin a minute you will be able to gamble for at least an hour and 40 minutes. If you bet 10 chips per spin you could lose your money in 10 minutes.

The ideal is to determine in advance how much you intend to spend and how long you would like to play for, and then place bets at a stake level and frequency that will allow you to enjoy your gaming.

On roulette, although it is tempting to bet on every spin, players are not obliged to do so and you will have more time to think if you bet less frequently. On blackjack you may also bet on another player's hand. While learning the game, this is a good tactic as it offers a useful way of gaining experience if you are not yet confident in your ability to play.

TOP *Elaborate architectural themes and the promise of instant riches draw gamblers to casinos around the world.*

Games
of Chance

Games of chance involve mechanical equipment and therefore have an element that the player cannot control. Slot machines and roulette are the most popular and widely played casino games as they appeal both to novices and more experienced players.

Casinos in Europe have a long tradition of playing roulette, but the game is less popular in the USA, where the casino has a bigger house advantage due to the addition of an extra zero. Apart from this amendment, roulette has remained virtually unchanged for hundreds of years.

Slots account for more than 60 per cent of gaming revenues in American casinos. This is because slots are easy to play and offer potentially huge returns for a relatively small stake. New technology constantly produces more sophisticated games.

AMERICAN ROULETTE

⦿ American roulette, which is played with two zeros, is derived from the original French version, played with only one zero.

Casinos like the American version because it is less expensive to run than French roulette and only needs one dealer to operate the game. American roulette is also more profitable as the bets come flooding in at a faster rate.

⦿ American roulette is played on a large table which is printed with a betting layout. At one end of the table a wheel encased in a wooden cylinder turns on a spindle.

The wheel is divided into 38 sections, numbered from zero to 36 inclusive, plus a section numbered double zero (00).

Consecutive numbers are arranged opposite each other on the wheel. Each number is coloured either red or black and the zeros are coloured green.

The aim of roulette is to predict the number on which a ball spun around the wooden cylinder will land. The ball is spun by hand by a dealer and must make at least three revolutions before dropping into one of the numbered sections on the wheel. The ball moves in the opposite direction to which the wheel is spun. Each new spin starts from the previous number.

ABOVE AND OPPOSITE *Each player uses differently coloured chips and each table has its own set of chips with a unique design.*

⦿ Roulette chips can only be used on the table to which they correspond. Their value is automatically the minimum bet on that table. If players want the chips to have a higher value they simply inform the dealer, who will position markers to denote the chips' new value, which may be up to the table maximum.

⦿ Although roulette players may bet with cash chips, it is advisable to play with table chips (also called 'colour') to avoid disputes. If a player does start betting with cash chips the dealer will call out, for example, 'reds on' or 'blacks on', depending on the value of the chips. This warns other players not to bet with the same colour cash chips.

● The dealer controls the running of the game by giving a number of specific verbal instructions which indicate each stage of the game. To ensure their bets are correctly placed, players should listen carefully to the dealer. If a player happens to accidentally knock another player's chip out of position, the dealer will straighten up the bet and announce that a chip has been moved by calling out the colour and the position where it has been placed. There is a strict rule that one player may not touch another player's chips.

PLACING BETS

Although the betting layout looks complicated, placing bets is quite simple. To bet on individual numbers the chip is placed directly on top of the number. For two adjacent numbers on the layout, placing a chip on the middle of the line that divides them makes the bet. A bet on red or black, high or low, even or odd is made by placing a chip in the corresponding box on the betting layout.

Casinos use both left- and right-hand tables, which adds to the confusion of placing bets. On a right-hand table the first column is the one furthest from the dealer, on a left-hand table it is closest to the dealer. Some of the basic bets that can be played are illustrated opposite. The colour in brackets refers to the appropriate chip on the diagram.

▶ Straight up (Green)

This is a bet on any one of the 38 numbers including 0 and 00. The chip should be placed directly on top of the desired number on the layout, ensuring that it is not touching any of the surrounding lines. It wins only if that number is spun.

▶ Split (Pink)

A bet on two adjacent numbers on the layout. The bet is placed on the centre of the line between the two numbers. It wins if either of the two numbers is spun.

▶ Street (Brown)

A bet on three adjacent numbers across the layout. It wins if any of the numbers is spun.

▶ Corner (Orange)

A bet on four adjacent numbers on the layout. The chip is placed on the line where they meet. It wins if any of the four numbers is spun.

▶ First four (Red)

A bet on the numbers 0, 1, 2, and 3. It is placed on the corner of the layout where 3 and 00 meet. It wins if any of the four numbers win.

▶ First five (Dark blue)

On a double-zero table, a bet on 0, 00, 1, 2 and 3. It is placed on the lines where 0, 00 and 2 meet. It wins if any of these numbers are spun.

▶ Double street (Purple)

A bet on six adjacent numbers across the layout. The chip is placed on the double line at the side of the layout at the cross section of the middle line of the six numbers.

▶ Quatro (Not shown)

Some layouts incorporate bets on a quarter of the numbers. The first quarter is numbers 1–9 inclusive, the second 10–18, the third

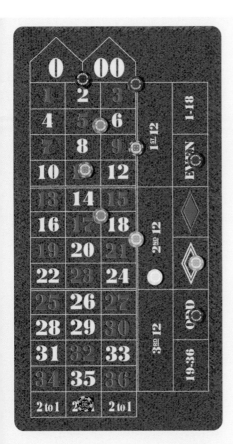

19–27, and the fourth 28–36. Bets are placed in the appropriate box. Bets lose if 0 is spun.

▶ Column (Black and grey stripes)

A bet on a group of 12 numbers running in one of the three columns along the table. Bets are placed in the box at the base of the column. The bet wins if any number in the column is spun. All bets on the column lose if 0 is spun.

▶ Dozen (Yellow)

A bet on a group of 12 consecutive numbers. There are three dozens: 1–12, 13–24 and 25–36 inclusive. Bets are placed in the appropriate box. The bet wins if any of the 12 numbers is spun. All bets on the dozens lose if 0 is spun.

▶ Even chance bets (Magenta and Blue)

Also called the outside bets, these are bets on a certain characteristic of the number spun, such as whether it is red or black, even or odd, high or low. Bets are placed in boxes marked with that characteristic and win if the appropriate one is spun. If 0 or 00 is spun, players lose half their stake.

TOP LEFT *Some of the most popular bets on roulette are illustrated in this layout.*

Predicting the winning number

Players have a wide range of bets from which to choose. The highest paying bet is to predict in which number the ball will land. Since there are 38 numbers on the wheel, this is also the most risky type of bet. The bets with the least risk (and the lowest return) are the even chances: bets on whether the ball will land on red or black, or on an odd or even, high or low number.

PLAYING THE GAME

▶ Before starting to play roulette, players first need to buy table chips. These can be purchased with money, cash chips or, in some casinos, with a personal cheque (check). Although bets may be placed using cash chips or money, it is advisable to always take a colour so that your bets are not confused with another player's bets.

The value of the colour chips will be marked on the table. The chips are stacked in piles of 20. Each set of colour comprises 200 chips. To prove that there are 20 chips in each stack, the dealer will cut the chips down into four piles of five chips and spread out one of the piles. The dealer will push the chips across the table to you.

▶ When you arrive at the table there will probably be a game in progress. The best time to buy chips is when the dealer announces 'place your bets'. Put your money or cash chips in front of you on the table and say 'colour'. If you want to cash a cheque, inform the dealer. Never place

money or cash chips for buying colour directly on the layout, as it will be assumed that you are making a bet. The dealer will take your money, count it and pass you the appropriate number of chips. If you have a preference for a particular colour you may ask for it, as long as no other player is using it already. You can then begin betting.

▶ Take care when placing bets. You may intend to bet straight up but if your chip is touching the line it may be assumed that it is a split. If other players have already placed bets on the numbers you want, simply put your chip on top of theirs. Never move another player's chips. If a player's bet is badly placed and you want to bet on that number, inform the dealer who will query the bet with the other player.

RIGHT *Here the dealer has cut the chips down into three piles of 20, then cut down one of them into four stacks of five chips with the last stack spread out on the table.*

several players have different preferences the highest-staking player usually takes precedence). Some casinos alternate the spin between clockwise and anti-clockwise turns to make it less likely that the ball will land in the same area of the wheel.

Occasionally a no-spin will be clearly announced if the ball makes fewer than three revolutions or the dealer makes a mistake in spinning the ball. The dealer will attempt to catch the ball but if he or she misses and the ball happens to land in a number it will not count as a winning number.

▶ When a game gets really busy it can become difficult to see the numbers as they are all covered in chips. If you are not sure where a number is, ask the dealer to place your bet. Simply place your chip in front of you on the table and announce loudly and clearly what you want to bet on. The dealer will repeat your instructions and place the bet on your behalf.

A short while before the ball drops into the wheel the dealer will announce 'no more bets', and any bets placed after this may be refused. Once the ball has settled the dealer announces the winning number, winning colour and whether it is odd or even. A marker, called a dolly, is placed on top of the chips on the winning number. All losing bets are cleared away. Occasionally winning bets are removed in error. If this happens, tell the dealer, who will then summon the inspector. As the action on the tables is recorded any claims can be verified.

Spinning the ball

When the players are almost finished placing bets, the dealer will spin the ball. The starting point of the spin is the last number spun. The first spin of the day is spun from the date. So on 6 July the first spin of the ball will be from number six. If the table is very busy, the dealer will make a long spin. On a quieter table the spin will be shorter. Players may request a long or short spin (if

TOP LEFT *The dealer places a marker, called a dolly, on top of the winning chips so they are not swept away in error.*

❶ Player places money, or cash chips, on the table and calls for colour.

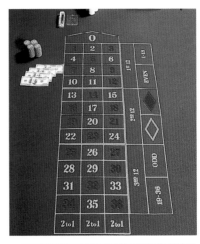

❷ Dealer counts the money or cash chips, and passes the player the appropriate number of table chips.

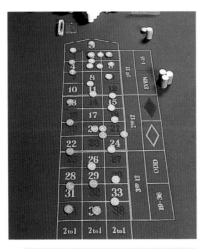

❸ Dealer announces 'place your bets'. When bets are placed, dealer spins ball and announces 'no more bets'.

❹ Number 20 wins. Dealer announces 'twenty, black, even', and places a marker (dolly) on 20.

5 Dealer clears away losing bets and calculates the winning payouts.

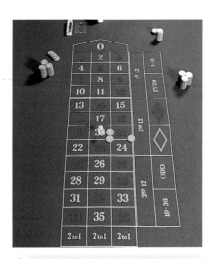

6 One player has a winning bet straight up, a split, a corner and a double street. Total = 65 chips.

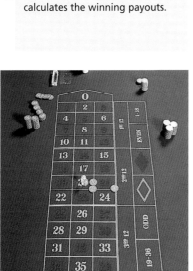

7 The dealer proves the payout by cutting down a stack and then spreading the other five chips.

8 The winning chips are passed to the player. The dealer announces 'place your bets'.

GAMES OF CHANCE

Bets on dozens are paid at 2 to 1.

Even chance bets are paid at 1 to 1.

A winning column is paid at 2 to 1.

Winning bets

Winning bets are paid out in a set order, starting with the winning column, even chances and winning dozen. Then the bets around the number are paid. One player may be fortunate enough to have several winning bets. These will be totalled and paid together. For each colour, the dealer will announce the number of chips won and prepare the payout. The dealer judges how many colour chips the player needs to continue playing and will make up the rest of the payout with cash chips. Players can request to have their payout made up however they like.

▶ If you need more colour chips or more cash chips, tell the dealer. If you want to stop playing, however, ask for cash chips. Always check your payout as mistakes do get made. Queries should be addressed to the inspector.

▶ If zero is spun, the bets associated with zero are paid out as normal, but half of the stake from the even chances is lost and will be removed by the dealer.

▶ When all the bets have been paid out, the dealer will remove the dolly and announce 'place your bets'. This is the cue for players to start betting once again. All winning bets are left in place, so if you do not want to bet on the same numbers again you must remember to remove your chips yourself.

STRATEGY

What are the payout odds?

▶ **Straight up**
Odds paid are 35 to 1 (also written as 35/1).

▶ **Split**
Odds paid are 17 to 1

▶ **Street**
Odds paid are 11 to 1.

▶ **Corner**
Odds paid are 8 to 1.

▶ **First four**
Odds paid are 8 to 1.

▶ **First five**
Odds paid are 6 to 1.

▶ **Double street**
Odds paid are 5 to 1.

▶ **Quatro**
Odds paid are 3 to 1.

▶ **Column**
Odds paid are 2 to 1.

▶ **Dozen**
Odds paid are 2/1.

▶ **Even chance bets**
Odds paid are evens.

On roulette the number of zeros on the wheel affects the house advantage. A wheel with two zeros has a house advantage of 5.26 per cent. A wheel with one zero has an advantage of 2.7 per cent. It is therefore more profitable from a player's point of view to bet on a wheel with only one zero. This house advantage applies to all bets with the exception of the outside bets and the five-number bets on American roulette. The outside bets (high, low, odd, even, black and red) have the lowest house advantage. In British casinos when zero is spun on a one-zero wheel, half the stake from all outside bets is lost. These bets have a house advantage of 1.35 per cent.

FRENCH ROULETTE

• French roulette, the predecessor of the American version, is mostly played in European casinos and is dealt in French. Although the equipment and language used differs, it is in principle the same game as American roulette, although it is played more slowly.

• The dealers move the chips using a stick, called a rake. Players bet by throwing their chips to roughly the correct place and the dealers then line them up using the rake.

• Although the game is dealt in French, players familiar with American roulette can get by with just a few words of French.

❶ *Voisins du zéro*
❷ *Les orphelins*
❸ *Tiers du cylindre*

French roulette is played on a table roughly twice the size of that used for American roulette. The betting layout differs, the numbers are arranged in a random order and there is only one zero. Each table has two dealers and a *chef de table* (inspector), who are all seated around the wheel.

SPECIALITY BETS

Unlike American roulette, some of the bets placed on French roulette cover particular sections of the wheel.

▶ Tiers du cylindre

Commonly called *tiers*. A six-chip bet consisting of splits covering numbers 5/8, 10/11, 13/16, 23/24, 27/30, 33/36. This bet covers almost one-third of the wheel, from 33 to 27.

▶ Voisins (Neighbours bet)

A bet on five numbers straight up that are adjacent to one another on the wheel. A bet on '*cinq et les voisins*' (five and the neighbours) is a bet on number 5 and the two numbers either side of it on the wheel (a straight up on 23, 10, 5, 24 and 16).

▶ Voisins du zéro *(below left)*

A nine-chip bet that covers the section of the wheel around zero. The bets placed are 0/2/3 (2 chips) street. Splits on 4/7, 12/15, 18/21, 19/22, 32/35 and a four-number bet 25/26/28/29 (2 chips).

▶ Les orphelins *(below right)*

Les orphelins, or the orphans, covers the sections of the wheel that are not covered by the tiers and '*voisins du zéro*'. It is a five-chip bet on number 1 straight and the splits 6/9, 14/17, 17/20, 31/34.

STRATEGY

What are the payout odds?

⊳ Tiers du cylindre
If any number in the section from 33 to 27 is spun, 17 chips are won and five chips are lost.

⊳ Voisins du zéro
If 0, 2, 3, 25, 26, 28 or 29 are spun, 16 chips are won and 8 lost. If any other number is spun, 17 chips are won and 8 are lost.

⊳ Voisins
Payout odds are 35/1. If any of the five numbers is spun, 35 chips are won and four chips are lost.

⊳ Les orphelins
If 1 is spun, 35 chips are won and 3 chips lost. However, if number 17 wins then 34 chips are won and 3 chips are lost. If either 6, 9, 14, 20, 31 or 34 are spun, 17 chips are won and 4 chips are lost.

TOP RIGHT *Monte Carlo Casino is one of many European casinos that offer the French version of roulette. The forerunner of American roulette, this popular game, which translates as 'little wheel' in French, is the oldest of all modern casino games, dating back almost 300 years.*

HOUSE ADVANTAGE

The house advantage on all inside bets depends on the zeros on the wheel. With one it is 2.7 per cent and with two it is 5.26 per cent. Multiple bets on French roulette consist of inside bets with a house advantage of 2.7 per cent. For example, a *voisin* has a house advantage value of five '*en pleins*' and each **en plein** has a house advantage of 2.7 per cent.

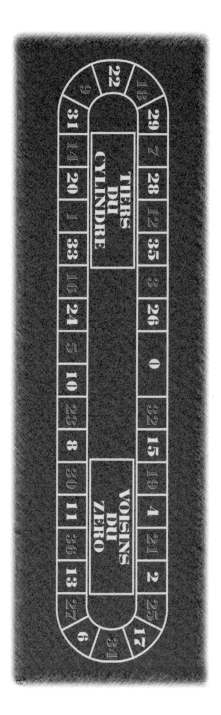

ENGLISH ROULETTE

● This is a hybrid of American and French roulette. To confuse matters even more, the English call it American roulette. English Roulette is mostly played in British and European casinos on American roulette tables using the French wheel (one zero).

● The game is similar to American roulette but incorporates many elements of French roulette as well, including French terms for the bets as well as the speciality bets of *voisins*, *tiers* and *orphelins*.

Neighbours oval

Some English roulette tables have a neighbours oval: a diagram of the wheel printed on the layout in front of the dealer. It allows neighbour bets to be placed quickly and efficiently.

In order to play this game give the dealer five chips and announce your bet clearly. For 'five and the neighbours', the dealer will place the chips on the number 5 on the oval. The ball is spun and the dolly placed. The dealer will point to the winning number on the oval and announce either 'neighbours win' or 'neighbours lose'. If there is a winning neighbour bet, a chip is subsequently removed from the oval, placed on the successful number and paid out to the player as a winning straight-up bet.

RAPID ROULETTE

In 2000 a new form of roulette was introduced called Rapid roulette. It was based on the game of Aussie roulette, a slot machine version of the game played in Australian casinos.

Aussie roulette was not particularly popular with traditional roulette players because they preferred the human factor of having a dealer spin the ball. In 1999, Crown Casino Australia and Stargames, an Australian gaming equipment and technology company, developed a semi-automated version of roulette that combined elements of both traditional and Aussie roulette.

▶ The equipment

The hybrid, Rapid roulette makes use of a traditional roulette wheel and dealer to generate the winning numbers, with the dealer also handling buy-ins.

The baize betting layout has been replaced with state-of-the-art computer terminals arranged around the roulette table. This system allows for bets to be placed without the pushing and shoving associated with traditional roulette, and also allows for varied stakes.

▶ How to play

To start playing, on-screen chips are bought from the dealer. To make a bet, players touch on a chip and drag it to the correct betting position. A timer indicates how long a player has left to do so. The dealer spins the roulette wheel. The winning number is entered into a console and the winning bets are automatically calculated and paid by the computer. To stop playing, the 'cash-out' button is pressed. The dealer then pays out the number of on-screen chips to the player.

▶ Placing bets

Traditional roulette bets can be played. In addition, there are mystery jackpots, progressives, quick picks, quinellas and trifectas. Rapid roulette has soared in popularity and is now played in many renowned casinos around the world.

ABOVE *English Roulette incorporates elements of French Roulette, particularly the French terms for bets as seen on this cash chip,* **voisins du zero**.

WINNING ROULETTE IN A NUTSHELL

▶ Every casino has its loyal band of system hunters – players who sit for hours at the roulette tables noting the winning numbers spun and analyzing the results, all hoping for a winning formula. Casinos even supply these dedicated people with paper and pencils for this purpose, confident in the knowledge that the variables make this task virtually impossible.

▶ There are a number of elements of roulette that are designed to make the prediction of the winning number more difficult, such as the deflection bars, the speed of the wheel and the ball, and whether the wheel is positioned on a left- or right-handed table. The easiest way to eliminate all these variations on roulette is to concentrate pointedly on what each dealer is doing.

▶ The winning number can quite often be predicted by analyzing a dealer's spins. Each dealer has a unique spin and, although he is trained to spin the ball at different speeds, in practice this doesn't always happen and it is fairly common for previous numbers to be repeated, sometimes up to five times in a row. For many dealers, this is usually a wake-up call to change their spin. The pit staff are also trained to be alert to dealers spinning neighbours bets and will give them a quick warning to change their spin.

▶ By recording the spins a particular dealer makes and analyzing the data collected, it is possible to find dealers with consistent spins. You can then follow the dealer round the tables for an entire shift and place bets based on your predictions. This will mean, however, that you may need to have a sufficient bankroll to place bets on the higher staking tables.

▶ The easiest way to find a dealer with a consistent spin is to count the number of revolutions the ball makes. For example, you may find that a dealer's spin averages seven revolutions. You then need to analyze where the ball lands on these spins, record the number of revolutions it makes, as well as the starting point (the last winning number) and the finishing point (the winning number). You then need to eliminate any spins that are longer or shorter than the average spin (seven in this case) and estimate the distance between the starting point and the winning number. You may, for instance, find that the ball travels an average of five numbers further. You can then use this information to predict the winning number and place your bets on a block of numbers around your prediction. Neighbours bets or speciality bets are ideal for this method of play. You need to take into account left- and right-handed tables as they will give different results.

SPIN AND WIN

In addition to roulette, which is an all-time favourite pastime in gambling halls all over the world, there are a number of other popular casino games that are played using spinning wheels. Many of these echo the original fairground wheel of fortune that has become the forerunner of today's mechanical games.

BOULE

Like roulette, boule players bet where a ball will land on a spinning wheel. The wheel has a series of indentations marked with four sets of the numbers one to nine. Bets include single numbers, the colours red and black, high and low numbers, and even and odd numbers. The number five has the same role as the zero on roulette.

BIG SIX WHEEL

Big six wheel is a simple game played with a large spinning wheel which stands vertically and is spun by the dealer. Almost any number of players can participate. The wheel is covered with symbols and payout amounts. The aim is to predict where the wheel will stop. The betting layout is marked with boxes that correspond with the sections of the wheel. Bets are made by placing chips in the relevant number box. In Australia, a similar game is called Big Money Wheel.

In America the wheel has 54 sections, in Australia it has 52. The Australian wheel has a house advantage of 7.69 per cent on all bets. The house advantage on an American wheel varies with different bets. Also, better odds are paid for the joker/logo bet in Atlantic City.

PAYOUT ODDS AND HOUSE ADVANTAGE

American wheel

$1	Even	11.11%
$2	2/1	16.67%
$5	5/1	22.22%
$10	10/1	18.52%
$20	20/1	22.22%
Joker/Logo	40/1	24.07%
(In Atlantic City	45/1	14.81%)

Australian wheel

$1	Even	7.69%
$3	3/1	7.69%
$5	5/1	7.69%
$11	11/1	7.69%
$23	23/1	7.69%
Joker/Logo	47/1	7.69%

KENO

Keno is basically a continuous lottery. It is popular in American casinos, with many games played each day. Players choose from one to 10 numbers, which they mark onto a ticket (card). They present their ticket to a keno writer along with the appropriate stake and are issued with a computerized ticket. For each game, 20 numbers are randomly drawn and displayed on boards around the casino. The payouts for different combinations of numbers are also displayed. Players need to simply look at the board and check their ticket to find out if they have a win for the game they played.

Keno is played with small stakes but for potentially huge jackpots. An example of this is the 1998 win, at Burswood Casino in Australia, by a woman who won A$1 million for a A$2 bet.

HOUSE ADVANTAGE

The house advantage and payout odds vary in different casinos. Each casino has a printed copy of its odds and payout rules. It is best to scrutinize these before playing. The house advantage is typically around 29–30%. This high house advantage makes it one of the least profitable games to play; however, the attraction is the potentially huge payouts.

PAYOUT ODDS

The payout depends on the number of correct numbers selected. The more numbers you correctly select, the higher the payout. Picking one number correctly will typically enable players to win approximately $3. Players selecting 10 correct numbers can win a jackpot of $1 million in some casinos.

Games like keno prove that it is not always the good gamblers who win lots of money. An Australian from Townsville who won the biggest keno jackpot in Queensland did so without picking a single winning number. He had played two 'quick picks' at a local hotel. Simply because none of his 40 numbers came up, he automatically won A$250,000.

SLOTS

Most slot machines mimic traditional fruit machines, with basic symbols on spinning drums, but instead of the original three drums many now incorporate five drums, or payout lines, making it harder for players to win. Each coin played brings a new line into play, so it makes sense to play the maximum number of lines per spin. Mechanical systems, which used rotating drums and were activated by pulling a lever, have given way to push-button-operated microprocessor-controlled machines with all payouts administered by computer chips but there is no changing the popularity of the slots.

The object of playing the slots is to spin the drums so that identical symbols end up across the winning line (either vertically or horizontally). There is a hierarchy of symbols, with some giving higher payouts than others. There are also differences in the way the payouts are calculated. Instructions for playing are printed on every slot machine, together with the relevant payout odds. Small amounts are paid out directly by the machines. However, if a large jackpot is won, it will be paid by a member of the casino's staff.

RIGHT *Banks of slot machines are often linked to a progressive jackpot, which increases every time a machine is played.*

Slots are traditionally played using either coins or metal tokens which are purchased at the cash point. Coinless slots are becoming increasingly popular nowadays and many new establishments – such as Sun International's GrandWest Casino in Cape Town, South Africa, are dispensing with coins altogether in favour of cards. A voucher or smart card (which looks like a credit card) is purchased which can be used on all the slot machines in that casino.

Card-based systems (*see* photograph above) have resulted in the creation of loyalty programmes for regular customers, who can build up points which can be exchanged for complimentary items such as accommodation and meals.

The latest innovations are adventure-style video slots that are based on arcade games. State-of-the-art computer graphics and cutting-edge technology create realistic

images, sound and animation, while fantasy designs encourage players to move from one machine to the next in the hope of hitting the jackpot.

There are also video slots that imitate table games like poker. These are popular with less confident players, as they allow one-on-one betting against the machine instead of placing bets at a crowded table.

BELOW *Slot machines are the casino's mainstay, offering the chance of instant riches to the lucky few.*

STRATEGY

Slot machines (slots) are by far the easiest and most popular casino games to play because they require no skill on the part of the players. They also offer potentially huge returns for a small investment. There is an infinite variety of machines.

Treble-, double-& single-bars

There are a variety of symbols used on slots. These can be 7s, treble-bars, double-bars, single-bars, stars and bells as well as fruit symbols such as melons, oranges and cherries. The value of the symbols depends entirely on the machine being played and each machine has its own hierarchy of symbols.

Symbol combinations

A table showing the payouts for each combination of symbols is marked on the machine. Always study the payout table before playing, as the lowest ranked symbols on some machines can be the highest on others and vice-versa. For example, on some machines you will need a line of 7s to hit the jackpot, on others it may be a line of cherries. Some machines include a symbol that can be used like a wild card. This symbol will only apply to the particular machine being playing.

Some machines allow you to hold one or more of these wild cards while the remainder of the reels spin. If it is possible to hold such a symbol, the 'hold' button will flash. To hold the symbol simply press this button and it will then stop flashing. Conversely, to cancel a hold simply press the button again.

The highest recorded slot win is $39,713. It was won on 21 March, 2003 at the Excalibur Hotel and Casino in Las Vegas. The winner, a 25-year-old software engineer from Los Angeles, chose to remain anonymous. He won the jackpot after making bets totalling $100 on the $1 Nevada Megabucks machine.

HOUSE ADVANTAGE

The house advantage varies from approximately 1.5–9%. The payout of the machine is often given as a percentage of the stakes the machine returns and can sometimes be as high as 98.5%. To find the highest paying machines on the casino floor ask the staff on duty. Remember that although the payout is shown at 98.5% this only comes into effect over a long period of play. If you bet $100 this does not necessarily guarantee you will win back $98.5 immediately.

GAMES OF CHANCE

Counting your Cards

Blackjack, which is based on the card game 21 or pontoon, is one of the most popular table games due to the fact that players do not have to rely on luck alone. Instead, it is the way they play that determines whether they win or lose. Computer simulations that have calculated the best strategies for winning demonstrate that it is possible to overcome the casino's advantage. To achieve this means memorizing the best action to take, depending on the cards that are dealt, but players who master the skill have a realistic chance of winning.

BLACKJACK

- Blackjack is always played against the dealer, who plays on the casino's behalf. The main aim is to draw cards that will beat the dealer's hand without exceeding a score of 21. Standard decks of 52 cards are used (jokers are not used) and the total number of decks does not affect the game. Six decks are most often used, giving a total of 312 cards in play.

Blackjack is played on a semi-circular table which is operated by a dealer who quickly and efficiently shuffles and deals the decks of cards, pays out winning bets and collects losing bets. There are places at the table for up to seven players. A player may play more than one hand at a time, with each hand counting as a separate bet against the dealer.

TOP RIGHT *A shuffled pack is cut by inserting a blank card into the deck to indicate when it should be reshuffled.*

RIGHT *Blackjack tables await players in the elegant sumptuously decorated Monte Carlo Casino.*

• Although some casinos use machines, the cards are mostly shuffled by hand. After shuffling, the dealer will invite a player to cut the cards. To deter card counters, a card is removed from the top of the deck and placed in the discard pile. Players start by making an initial bet. One card is then dealt face up to each player and face down to the dealer, followed by a second card dealt face up to each player as well as to the dealer. The players add up the value of the cards they hold and try to assess the potential score of the dealer's hand before making their next moves. The objective is to achieve a total closer to 21 than the dealer's cards but not to exceed 21 (in which case the player loses).

Doubling your bet

Doubling is restricted to the first two cards dealt and players are then allowed only one further card to each hand. The double bet is made by placing chips behind the original bet after the first two cards are dealt to a player's hand. Winning bets are paid at odds of evens. Rules vary in different casinos so enquire before making this type of bet.

SCORING

The card values in each player's hand are added to give the scores. Cards from 2–10 inclusive have their face value. Court cards (kings, queens and jacks) are worth 10. Aces have an initial value of 11, decreasing to 1 if the hand subsequently exceeds a score of 21. Blackjack, the highest hand possible, is an ace plus any card worth 10. Only the first two cards dealt can make blackjack. Cards dealt to a split hand (see p52) do not count.

Queen (10) & ace (11) is blackjack (21).

King (10) & 10 give a score of 20.

7 & 8 give a score of 15.

Ace (11) & 8 is 19. If a 2 is dealt, this becomes 21.

COUNTING YOUR CARDS

BEGINNING THE GAME

Players may bet on as many boxes as they wish. They have the option of playing themselves or, in Europe and some other countries, betting on another player's hand. This is useful if you are a novice and not yet confident of your own skills.

The second player bets by placing his chip next to the original bet. The first player has, as a result, complete control over the hand and all subsequent action taken. If a hand is split the second player does not have to make an additional bet but may nominate, instead, which hand he would like to bet on. Similarly, the second player does not have to double if the original player doubles.

Where to place bets

After making their initial bets by placing chips in the boxes marked on the layout, the players are dealt two cards face up. The dealer also receives two cards, only one of which is revealed to the players (the up card). The dealer's other card (the hole card) remains face down on the table.

After assessing the value of their hands, players can choose from a selection of options – depending on the value of their own hands and the dealer's up card – to enable them to beat the dealer without going over 21.

▶ Stand (Green chip)

Take no further cards.

▶ Hit (Purple chip)

Players take one or more cards to improve their score. The procedure for asking for another card varies from country to country. In the USA it is common practice to tap the table to hit (take another card) and to wave your hand (or move it horizontally) to pass (not accept another card).

In the UK the dealer will ask each player in turn if he or she wants another card, and the player simply replies 'yes' or 'no'. In the event of a dispute or misunderstanding, players should refer to the inspector.

▶ Split (Red chips)

This occurs when the first two cards drawn are the same (in this instance two kings). The player splits the hand by placing another bet on the line of the box. With aces, only one more card may be dealt to each hand but on any other split, players can draw as many cards as required. Splits can only score 21, not blackjack.

▶ Double (Blue chips)

Sometimes players may double their bet by increasing it to twice the initial stake. Players do not have to double the initial stake, but may make an additional bet up to the total value of the initial bet (see p51).

*The colours of the discs in the diagram above are illustrative only and are not part of the game plan.

- If a player's score exceeds 21, he or she loses and the dealer clears the cards. Even if the dealer's hand exceeds 21, the player still loses, but this isn't counted as a stand-off (a tie between the dealer and player).

- Players stand (take no more cards) when they are satisfied they have sufficient cards to beat the dealer's eventual score. When all the players have indicated that they are standing, the dealer plays his or her hand by revealing the down card (the hole card).

- The casino's rules determine the action to be taken by the dealer based on the total of the two cards. If the dealer's cards add up to 17 or over, he or she must stand. With a score of 16 or less, the dealer is obliged to take additional cards until the

total exceeds 16. If the dealer's score goes above 21, the house loses and the players' winning bets are paid out.

- If the dealer's score is below 21, players with higher scores win and are paid out. If the score is a stand-off (a tie) on blackjack or any other total, the bet is not lost and the player's original stake is returned.

- When a player is dealt blackjack and the dealer cannot make blackjack, the player's winnings are paid out and the cards removed before any other cards are dealt. However if the dealer's up card is an ace or any card with a value of 10, the player with blackjack waits until all the other players' hands are played, as the dealer may have blackjack and therefore tie with the player.

Insurance

If the dealer's first card is an ace, he or she will ask the players if they want to take insurance. This is an additional bet, equal to half of the player's original stake, against the possibility of the dealer making blackjack. If the dealer subsequently does make blackjack, the original bet loses, but the insurance bet is paid at odds of 2 to 1. If the dealer does not have blackjack the insurance bet is lost and the original bet is paid out at 3 to 2.

Whatever the outcome of the dealer's hand, the net result is the same; even money is won.

If a player does decide to take insurance, most casinos immediately pay out the bet at evens and remove the player's cards from the table. Taking insurance is not generally considered a good bet, however, as the dealer's chances of making blackjack are outweighed by the chance of making any other scores.

ADDITIONAL BETS

Some casinos have introduced additional bets on blackjack. However they do not really offer good value and novices will find that it is better to concentrate on learning how to play the basic game well.

STRATEGIC MOVES

▶ **Surrender blackjack:** If a player is dealt a poor initial hand he or she may surrender half of their stake, which is removed by the dealer, and the player's hand is not played. However if the dealer has blackjack the entire stake is lost.

▶ **Over/under 13:** This is a bet that the first two cards dealt will be either over or under 13. The additional bet loses if the score is exactly 13. This bet is placed at the same time as the initial bet. Whatever the outcome of the additional bet, the hand is played out as normal.

STRATEGIC MOVES continued:

▶ **Multiple action blackjack**: The player keeps the same hand for three consecutive games and the dealer retains the same up card. The first two cards are dealt according to normal procedure and the player may draw on these cards. The dealer follows the normal rules and procedures for drawing cards (stands on 17 or over, draws on 16 or under). A good hand has an excellent chance of winning three times over. Conversely, a bad hand could lose three times in succession.

▶ **Three 7s:** A player is dealt three cards to the value of 7; the bet can be made at the same time as an initial bet is made.

TOP *Blackjack is dealt at high speed so players need to make quick calculations.*

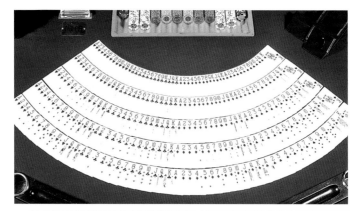

❶ Before the day's play begins, the dealer fans out the decks of cards in numerical sequence, suit by suit, to check that full decks are being used. The cards are also scrutinized to ensure that they are not marked or damaged in any way. All marked cards are removed and replaced immediately. This applies throughout play.

❷ The order of play is from the dealer's left (that is from right to left in the illustrations). Players place their initial bets in the boxes marked on the layouts. Two players are betting on box **E**. The second player places a bet below the first player's chip. Two cards are dealt face up to each player. The dealer receives two cards (one face up and the other, the hole card, face down).

❸ Player **A** has a score of 10 (6 + 4). Player **B** has blackjack (ace + jack) and is paid out immediately at 3:2 as the dealer's up card card (7) shows it is not possible to score blackjack. Player **C** has a score of 12 (first ace = 11, 2nd ace = 1). Player **D** has a score of 17. Player **E** has a score of 14.

❹ Players may now take extra cards.
Player **A** hits (calls for another card) and is subsequently dealt a 10, giving a total score of 20.
Player **A** decides to stand on that score.

❺ Player **C** decides to split. Each ace now becomes the first card on two separate hands, with a value of 11. Each new hand is dealt one more card. The first hand scores 17 (11 + 6) and the other 21 (11 + 10). This is not blackjack, as it has been made with a split hand.

❻ Player **D** decides to stand on his score of 17.
Player **E** hits (takes another card) and draws an 8, to end up with a total of 22. This is called a bust as the value of his cards exceeds 21.

7 The dealer removes player **E**'s stake and cards. The remaining players all decide to stand.

8 The dealer's second card is revealed as a king, giving the dealer a score of 17. Player **A** has a higher score (20) than the dealer, so wins and is paid odds of evens. Player **C** has a hand with the same score as the dealer. As this is a tie he keeps his stake. The other hand beats the dealer and is paid at odds of evens. Player **D** also has a tie and keeps the stake.

STRATEGY

Blackjack is a game where a player's individual skills can have an effect on his or her winnings. The average house advantage on blackjack is 5.6 per cent but there are ways that players can overcome this. Using computer programs to simulate games a system, known as basic strategy, has been developed which determines the best action for players to take according to the value of the cards they hold. By playing basic strategy, players can reduce the house advantage to zero. This involves memorizing the correct action to take for the cards dealt. In its simplest form, basic strategy means hitting on a score of 16 or lower if the dealer shows a 7 or above, and standing on a score of 12 or higher if the dealer shows 6 or lower.

The chart on page 62 shows basic strategy in more detail. It takes time to memorize but is worth studying if you intend to play blackjack seriously.

HOUSE ADVANTAGE

A classic technique for **reducing** the house advantage is card counting. The house advantage on blackjack is given as an average of 5.6 per cent because frequent card shuffling means the house advantage constantly changes.

There are times when the player has an advantage. This arises if more high value cards remain in the shoe. The dealer is then at a disadvantage due to the rules that determine when he or she must take further cards. Players can stand on any score but the dealer must hit on 16 or lower. Therefore the dealer has a much greater chance of busting if there are plenty of tens left in the shoe. Spotting when this happens is the basis for card counting.

PAYOUT ODDS

Payouts are calculated according to the value of the player's hand when compared with the dealer's hand. When a player has blackjack and beats the dealer, the odds paid are 3 to 2. A win pays even money. A stand off results in the original stake being returned.

If a player has taken insurance against the dealer making blackjack, the insurance bet will be paid out at 2 to 1 if this occurs.

OPPOSITE *Frequent shuffling of dealers' cards by hand or machine is just one of the many methods casinos use to deter very persistent game analysts.*

CARD COUNTERS

Accomplished card counters can have an advantage of between one and 1.5 per cent over the casino if card counting is combined with the basic strategy. Card counting techniques work by assigning a value to each card. As the cards are dealt, players keep a running count and when a certain level is reached, bets are increased. There are numerous methods that can be used but the simplest ones are often the best.

Becoming a good card counter takes a lot of practice and complete concentration. Learning to count several cards or whole hands at once improves the speed. It is best to practise at home until the various techniques have been properly mastered.

In one example of card counting, a running count is kept as the cards are dealt. Aces and cards with a face value of 10 are counted as minus one. Cards with a value of two to six inclusive are counted as plus one. When the count is positive, the player begins to increase his bets.

Avoid detection

Using the card-counting technique effectively is only half the battle, however. The other challenge is to avoid detection by the casino. Although card counting is not illegal, casinos do everything in their power to deter this practice. Players suspected of it are usually asked to leave.

Casinos also try to combat card counters by 'burning' cards (dealing a few cards unseen into the discard pile), adding more decks to the shoe, shuffling the cards frequently, and using shuffling machines.

A classic sign of card counting in action is a player making much higher bets in the second half of the shoe. Casino personnel are trained to look out for this and report it to pit bosses. Once spotted, a suspected card counter will be watched, often by the pit boss, but also from the camera room.

To go undetected be a small fish in a big pond. If the casino is busy, with lots of high

PLAYER'S HAND				DEALER'S UP CARD						
	2	3	4	5	6	7	8	9	10	Ace
8	H	H	H	H	H	H	H	H	H	H
9	H	D	D	D	D	H	H	H	H	H
10	D	D	D	D	D	D	D	D	H	H
11	D	D	D	D	D	D	D	D	D	H
12	H	H	X	X	X	H	H	H	H	H
13	X	X	X	X	X	H	H	H	H	H
14	X	X	X	X	X	H	H	H	H	H
15	X	X	X	X	X	H	H	H	H	H
16	X	X	X	X	X	H	H	H	H	H
17	X	X	X	X	X	X	X	X	X	X
18	X	X	X	X	X	X	X	X	X	X
19	X	X	X	X	X	X	X	X	X	X
20	X	X	X	X	X	X	X	X	X	X
21	X	X	X	X	X	X	X	X	X	X
Ace 2	H	H	H	D	D	H	H	H	H	H
Ace 3	H	H	H	D	D	H	H	H	H	H
Ace 4	H	H	D	D	D	H	H	H	H	H
Ace 5	H	H	D	D	D	H	H	H	H	H
Ace 6	H	D	D	D	D	H	H	H	H	H
Ace 7	X	X	X	X	X	X	X	H	H	H
Ace 8	X	X	X	X	X	X	X	X	X	X
Ace 9	X	X	X	X	X	X	X	X	X	X
Ace 10	X	X	X	X	X	X	X	X	X	X
Ace Ace	S	S	S	S	S	S	S	S	S	S
2 2	S	S	S	S	S	S	S	S	S	S
3 3	S	S	S	S	S	S	H	H	H	H
4 4	H	H	H	H	H	H	H	H	H	H
5 5	D	D	D	D	D	D	D	D	H	H
6 6	S	S	S	S	S	H	H	H	H	H
7 7	S	S	S	S	S	S	H	H	H	H
8 8	S	S	S	S	S	S	S	S	S	X
9 9	S	S	S	S	S	X	S	S	X	X
10 10	X	X	X	X	X	X	X	X	X	X

H = HIT   X = STAND   D = DOUBLE   S = SPLIT

rollers playing, all the attention will be on them and a player betting small stakes may be overlooked. Limiting the length of sessions means a player is less likely to be remembered. Avoid high denomination chips as these will attract attention. Don't put your winning chips on the table, and exchange them at frequent intervals.

If the pit boss starts watching you, continue playing for low stakes. The pit boss regularly checks each table's float. If you've suddenly won a lot of money, make yourself scarce. The inspector may not notice you winning small amounts, but the pit boss will realize this once the float is counted.

To evade detection, professional card counters work in a team and enter a casino separately. One starts playing blackjack for low stakes and counts the cards. The others wait for a signal that the shoe favours the players, and when it is given, the others join the game and play for high stakes. This can only be done once, as players are identified and a record kept of their big wins.

THE RATIO OF TENS TO OTHER CARDS

A complex, but accurate, way of overcoming the house advantage in blackjack is to identify when the shoe is rich in cards worth 10. To do this, one needs to calculate the ratio of other-value cards to the cards worth 10. This requires concentration and some degree of mental dexterity because you need to be able to keep two running totals in your head and be able to divide one by the other at regular intervals.

In a deck of cards, there are 16 cards worth 10 and 36 other-value cards. The ratio of other-value cards to tens is 36/16 or 2.25. When the ratio falls below this level, the remaining cards in the shoe will be rich in tens. When this point is reached, bets are increased. The starting point for counting depends on how many decks are used. If, for example, four decks are used, the counting begins at 64

for the 10s and 144 for the other-value cards. When eight decks are used the counting begins at 128 for the 10s and 288 for the other-value cards. The total score for the 10s is reduced by one each time a 10 is seen. The tally for the remaining cards is reduced by one each time they are seen. This sum is then divided by the total of 10s to find the ratio. When the ratio is under 2.25, bets are increased. When the ratio is above 2.25 bets are reduced.

Example
Unseen others = 120
Unseen tens = 30
Ratio = 120/30 = 4
This is more than 2.25 so bets are reduced.

Testing a Shooter's Wit

The rowdiest game in the casino is dice, also called craps, a fast and exciting game with a language of its own. Players shout, cheer, scream, curse and gesticulate. The shooters elaborately shake the dice, blow on them for luck and yell for them to fall on the desired score, while the stickman commentates incessantly. For novices, dice appears complicated due to the arrangement of the layout and the terminology used, but it is actually quite simple once the basic aim of the game is understood. Craps is extremely popular everywhere, not only because it is fun to play, but also because it is the best value game in the casino. The house advantage on some bets is less than one per cent.

Two-up is an Australian coin tossing game that is as noisy as craps. It is not a dice game, but since it involves throwing an object and betting on where it will land, it is included in this chapter. Two-up is very easy to play. Two coins are thrown into the air and players bet on whether they will land on heads or tails.

CRAPS

▶ Dice is played on a large rectangular table, about the size of a billiard (pool) table, which is in the form of a pit (see opposite page). Players stand or sit around the outside. Up to 24 players can bet on each table. An indented rail around the edge of the table is designed to hold players' chips. The walls at each end of the pit are covered in pyramid-shaped projections against which the dice are thrown. These deflect the dice, making it more difficult to predict the score. The other two walls are mirrored. The table is printed with two identical betting layouts, one at each end.

▶ Dice games are operated by two dealers, a stickman and an inspector. Each dealer controls the betting layout at one end of the table. The stickman controls the game by moving the dice with a long stick and placing the bets. The inspector sits between the two dealers and resolves any disputes.

The game is played with precision-made gaming dice, which differ from those used in board games. Gaming dice are perfect cubes with square (not rounded) edges. They are transparent and marked with spots which correspond to the numbers one to six inclusive. Two dice are used and the total of the spots showing on the uppermost faces gives the score.

▶ The players take turns to throw the dice. The person throwing the dice (the shooter) stands at one end of the table and is offered a number of dice by the stickman, from which the shooter selects two. To begin, the shooter must place a bet on either the pass line (also called the win line) or the don't pass (don't win) line.

▶ The shooter's first throw of the dice is called the 'come out roll'. The dice are thrown simultaneously and must hit the wall at the opposite end of the table. Each new shooter continues to throw the dice until there is a miss-out (a losing decision). When this happens, the player to the left of the present shooter becomes the new shooter. Players may decline to take this position, in which case the turn passes to the next player on the left.

▶ Players get irate if the dice hit another player's hands when they are thrown. It is important to pay attention to the game and to keep your hands well away from the table when the dice are rolled. If you want to place a bet and the shooter is about to throw the dice, place your chips in front of you and call out the bet to the dealer, who will make sure it gets on.

OPPOSITE *The large craps tables are often located in a separate area of the casino. Up to 24 players can bet on each table.*

SCORING

● Players bet on the score thrown by the shooter. The most basic bets are on a winning or a losing score. A score of 7 or 11 on the come out roll is a winning score and is called a natural. A score of 2, 3 or 12 is a losing score and is called craps. Any other score means a point is established.

● When a point is established, the shooter continues to throw the dice and attempts to repeat the original score made on the come out roll. If the original score is thrown before a 7, the point is made. This is a winning score, so bets on the pass line win and bets on the don't pass line lose. However, if a 7 is thrown before the point is made, it is a losing score. Bets on the don't pass line win and bets on the pass line lose.

If a natural (7 or 11) is thrown on the come out roll, the bets on the pass line win

and the bets on the don't pass line lose. If craps (2, 3 or 12) is thrown on the come out roll, the bets on the don't pass line win and the bets on the pass line lose.

> A marker, called a puck, shows the progress of the game. It is used so that when new players arrive at the table, they can immediately see what stage the game has reached.

● When the puck is in the 'don't come' box, with 'OFF' uppermost it denotes the next throw of the dice as the come out roll. When a point is made the puck is turned so that 'ON' is uppermost and it is placed in a numbered box linked to the point made.

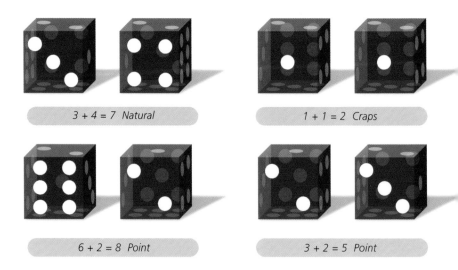

3 + 4 = 7 Natural

1 + 1 = 2 Craps

6 + 2 = 8 Point

3 + 2 = 5 Point

TYPES OF BETS

A wide choice of bets can be played on craps, some of which are better value for the player than others. Before betting, it is best to compare the difference in house advantage (the profit made by the casino) for each bet. The best-value bets are the pass/don't pass and come/don't come bets. These allow the player to make an additional bet called odds. By playing the odds bets, the house advantage is reduced to less than 1 per cent.

▶ Pass (win) line

Pass (win) bets must be placed before the come out roll and cannot be removed or reduced after the point is established. A bet on the pass line wins if a natural (7 or 11) is thrown on the come out roll or if a point is made. It loses if craps (2, 3 or 12) is thrown on the come out roll or if the shooter fails to make a point. Winning bets are paid at evens. This is the most common bet played. Players simply place the chips on the line in front of where they are standing.

▶ Don't pass (don't win) line

This bet must also be placed before the come out roll. After a point is established it can be reduced or removed. The bet wins if craps is thrown on the come out roll or if the shooter fails to make a point. It loses if a natural is thrown on the come out roll or if a point is made.

Casinos often bar either 2 or 12 to give themselves a bigger house advantage. A barred score is shown by two dice in the

don't pass section of the betting layout. The total score shown indicates the barred score. If two ones are shown then 2 is barred. If two sixes are shown, then 12 is barred. A barred score is void. This means it neither wins nor loses. A barred score is also known as a push or a tie.

▶ Come and don't come

Come and don't come bets are not very popular as many players do not understand how they work, but they allow players who join the game after the come out roll to bet.

Although they are similar to the bets made on the pass and don't pass lines, they differ in that they can be placed on any throw of the dice after the come out roll. When a player makes a come or don't come bet, the subsequent throw of the dice becomes the first throw for that particular bet.

The rules concerning whether the bet wins or loses are the same as those for the pass line bets. For example, if a come bet was placed on the third throw and the score is 6, the come bet will win if another score of 6 is thrown before a 7.

When a come or don't come bet is placed, the dealer moves the bet to the box of the score required. After a point is established, come bets cannot be reduced or removed. Don't come bets may be removed or reduced, however, after a point is established.

▶ Odds

These are additional bets that can be made once a point has been established, but the player must already have a bet on pass or don't pass, come or don't come. Odds bets are good value because they are paid out at true mathematical odds and no commission is charged. However casinos limit the amount that can be bet, varying from allowing a bet of up to the same amount as the original bet; to double the original bet; to a bet up to two and a half times the original stake.

The higher the stake a player can make on the odds bets, the lower the house advantage. Odds bets can be reduced or removed at any time.

On the come out roll, odds bets on the come line are off, but may be called on by the player. Odds bets on the don't come line are on at the come out roll. There is no specific area on the layout for these bets. The player makes the bet by placing additional chips behind his or her original pass or don't pass bet.

▶ Place

These are one of the most popular bets played in craps games and are bets made on the individual scores of 4, 5, 6, 8, 9 or 10. Place bets win if the score elected is thrown before a 7 is rolled. They can be made at any time. Place bets are off at the come out roll unless the player calls them on. The bets can be increased, decreased, removed or called off at any time. No commission is charged but place bets are paid out at less than the true mathematical odds.

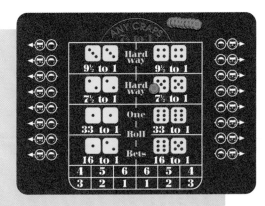

▶ Buy

These are similar to place bets, except that five per cent commission is paid to the house when the bet is placed. Winning buy bets are paid at true mathematical odds and may be increased, decreased or removed at any time with the commission adjusted accordingly. If a buy bet wins and it is left on again, a further five per cent commission is paid. Buy bets are off on the come out roll but may be called on by the player.

▶ Lay bets

Lay bets are the opposite of buy bets. If a 7 is rolled before the number on which a lay bet is placed, the bet wins and is paid at the true mathematical odds.

The bet loses if the nominated score is thrown after a 7 is rolled. Five per cent commission is charged on the amount the lay bet could win.

▶ Big six and big eight

A big six is a bet made on the shooter to throw a 6 before a 7. Similarly a big eight is a bet made on the chance that the shooter will throw an 8 before a 7. These bets are paid at odds of evens.

▶ Field

A field bet is a bet on just one roll of the dice. It pays odds of evens if any of the numbers 3, 4, 9, 10 or 11 are thrown, but the player loses the stake if 5, 6, 7 or 8 are rolled.

▶ Hardways (see illustration)

Hardways, or proposition, bets are for a score of 4, 6, 8 or 10 to be made with the same score on each dice. So hardway four is two 2s, hardway six is two 3s, hardway eight is two 4s and hardway 10 is two 5s. This bet wins if the nominated number is rolled as a pair before either a 7 is rolled or the nominated number is rolled 'easy' (the score is made with any combination of dice other than a pair). For example, a bet on hardways six will lose if a 6 is thrown that is made up of 2 and 4. Hardways bets are off on the come out roll but can be called on. They are placed on a separate layout in the centre of the craps table and the odds paid are printed on the hardways layout.

CRAPS BETS

Also known as proposition bets, crap bets are made against a single roll of the dice resulting in a specific score. A bet on any craps wins if a score of 2, 3 or 12 is thrown.

▶ Craps two
Wins if a score of 2 (1 + 1) is thrown with a single roll of the dice.

▶ Craps three
Wins if a score of 3 (2 + 1) is thrown.

▶ Craps twelve
Wins if a score of 12 (6 + 6) is thrown.

▶ Any seven
Wins if the next throw results in a score of 7 (3 + 4, 5 + 2 or 6 + 1).

▶ Eleven
Wins if a score of 11 (6 + 5) is thrown.

▶ Horn
Players make a combined bet on craps two, craps three, craps twelve and eleven. It is four separate bets on the numbers 2, 3, 11 and 12. The bet is made in multiples of four stake units.

▶ Horn high
Horn high is the same as a horn bet, plus an extra stake unit on a nominated number. Bets are made in multiples of five stake units and if a nominated number wins, the payout is doubled.

STRATEGY

Chances of throwing each score
There are 36 different combinations of dice that make up the scores (see illustration on p75). A score of 7 can be made in six different ways, while a score of 11 can be made in two ways. There is only one way to throw 2 or 12 and only two ways to throw a score of 3.

There are 24 different dice combinations by which a point (4, 5, 6, 8, 9 or 10) can be established. Players therefore have a reasonably good chance of either throwing a natural (7 or 11) or establishing a point on the come out roll.

ABOVE *A puck shows the progress of the game so that new players can assess what stage it has reached.*

HOUSE ADVANTAGE

▶ Pass (win) line
The house advantage is 1.41 per cent.

▶ Don't pass (don't win) line
If no numbers are barred, the house advantage is 1.4 per cent, rising to as high as 4.38 per cent if more than one number is barred.

▶ Come and don't come
On come the house advantage is 1.41 per cent while on don't come it is between 1.4 and 4.38 per cent.

▶ Odds
Scores of 4 and 10 give the house an advantage of 6.67 per cent; scores of 6 and 8 give 1.52 per cent; while 5 and 9 give 4 per cent.

▶ Buy
The house advantage is 4.76 per cent.

▶ Lay bets
Scores of 4 and 10 give a house advantage of 2.44 per cent; 5 and 9 give 3.23 per cent, and 6 and 8 give 4 per cent.

▶ Big six and big eight
The casino has a massive 9.09 per cent advantage. It is far better value to make a place bet on the 6 or the 8, which pays odds of 7 to 6 and gives a smaller house advantage of 1.52 per cent.

▶ Field
The house advantage is 5.5 per cent.

▶ Hardways
Scores of 4 and 10 give a house advantage of 11.11 per cent while 6 and 8 give 9.09 per cent.

▶ Craps bets
The house has an 11 per cent advantage.

▶ Craps two
The house has a 14 per cent advantage.

▶ Craps three
The house has an 11 per cent advantage.

▶ Craps twelve
The house has a 14 per cent advantage.

▶ Any seven
The house advantage is 16.67 per cent.

▶ Eleven
The house advantage is 11 per cent.

▶ Horn
The house advantage is 12,5 per cent.

▶ Horn high
On scores of 2 and 12, the house advantage is 12,78 per cent, on 3 and 11 it is 12,22 percent, while on any other number it is 16.67 per cent.

BET	PAYOUT ODDS	BET	PAYOUT ODDS
Pass line	evens	**Field**	
Don't pass line	evens	3, 4, 9, 10, 11	evens
Come	evens	2 or 12	2 to 1
Don't come	evens		
		Hardways	
Odds on pass line and come		4 or 10	7 to 1
4 or 10	2 to 1	6 or 8	9 to 1
5 or 9	3 to 2	Any seven	4 to 1
6 or 8	6 to 5	Any craps	7 to 1
		Craps two	30 to 1
Odds on don't pass line/don't come		Craps three	15 to 1
4 or 10	1 to 2	Eleven	15 to 1
5 or 9	2 to 3	Craps twelve	30 to 1
6 or 8	5 to 6		
		Horn	
Place bets (to win)		3 or 11	15 to 1
4 or 10	9 to 5	2 or 12	30 to 1
5 or 9	7 to 5		
6 or 8	7 to 6		
Buy bets			
4 or 10	2 to 1		
5 or 9	3 to 2		
6 or 8	6 to 5		

RIGHT *A stickman uses a curved stick to place chips on proposition numbers and to collect the dice after they have been thrown. He is also the voice of the craps table, disclosing the step-by-step progress of the game and announcing the winners and losers with each roll of the dice.*

DICE SETTING

Players can influence the winning number by setting the dice before they are thrown. Dice setting involves putting the dice in a preset position in your hand and controlling the way they are thrown so that they travel together along the table. The intention is that they will only rotate along the axis you have selected. For example, if you line up 5 on the top and 4 and 3 facing you and the dice rotate along their horizontal axis, the chances of throwing craps is eliminated.

Using this method allows you to have a greater chance of either throwing a natural or a point on the come-out roll. Other sets can be used to give players a greater chance of winning on other numbers. The numbers 4, 5, 9, 10, 2–2, 3–1 give only two possible sevens as do the numbers 2 or 12. This method will not guarantee that a particular number is thrown but with practice it can increase the chances. If you intend to use this technique, you need to learn to do it quickly so that the game is not held up. You can speed up the setting by practising at home. By experimenting with different types of throws and different grips, it is possible to find a technique that gives you the desired outcome more often than leaving it to chance. Even if you are unable to be an accomplished dice setter, you can look for other players that are using this technique and follow their bets.

The Crossed Hard 10

The Crossed Six

The Flying 'V' Set

The Hard 4

The Straight Sixes

The Hard 8

There is an increasing variety of different dice-set combinations. Some of the most popular combinations are indicated in the illustration on the opposite page. For each set, the first two numbers shown are the numbers on top of the dice.

The second two numbers are those on the sides facing towards you. An example of this is in the combination 5–5, 4–3. In this case, the dice are held in such a manner so that the two 5s are on top and the numbers 4 and 3 are facing you.

Similarly, in the 6–6, 2–2 combination, the two 6s are on top of the dice and the two 2s are facing you.

▶ For throwing sevens

The combination 5–5, 4–3 is good for the come-out roll, as it gives four possible sevens and no craps.

The combination 6–6, 2–2 gives four possible sevens and is good for bets of horns and hardways.

The combination 4–4, 6–6 gives four possible sevens and is good for the outside numbers.

▶ When a point is established

The combination 6–6, 5–4 gives only two possible 7s while the combination 3–3, 2–6 gives only two possible 7s.

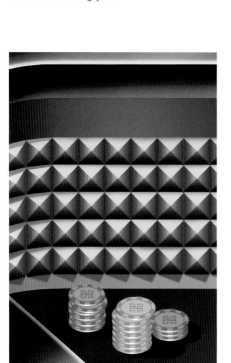

RIGHT *The pyramid-shaped projections on the end walls of the craps table help to deflect the dice, making it more difficult to predict how they will land.*

LEFT *Memorizing the following combinations of dice settings will better your chances of winning at craps:*
The crossed hard 10: 5–5, 4–3.
The straight sixes: 6–6, 2–2.
The hard 8: 4–4, 6–6.
The crossed six: 6–6, 5–4.
The flying V: 3–3, 2–6.
The hard 4: 2–2, 3–1.

Playing Craps

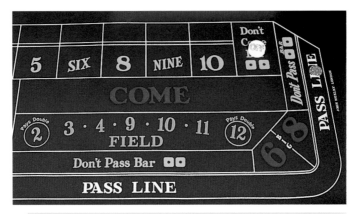

❶ Player **A**, the shooter, places a bet (blue chip) on the pass line. The puck in the don't come bar box, with 'off' showing, indicates that this is the come out roll.

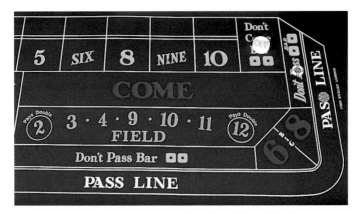

❷ Player **B** places a bet (white chip) on the don't pass line. If craps (2, 3 or 12) is thrown on the come out roll, this bet will win.

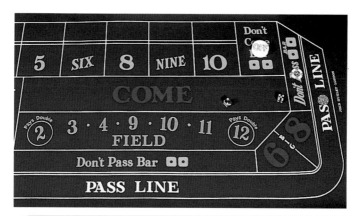

❸ The shooter (Player A) throws the dice. They land on a score of 7. As this is a natural, the bet on the pass line wins and the bet on the don't pass line loses.

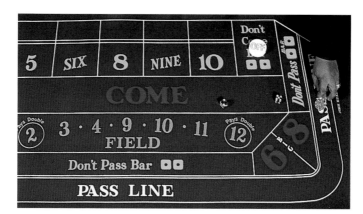

❹ Player A is paid out at evens for his bet on the pass line. Player B's bet on the don't pass line loses and his bet is cleared away by the dealer.

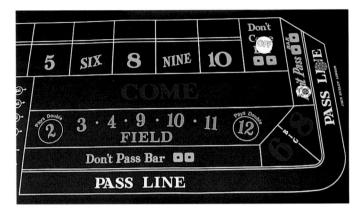

❺ Player **A** places another bet (blue chip) on the pass line.
Player **B** places another bet (white chip) on the don't pass line.

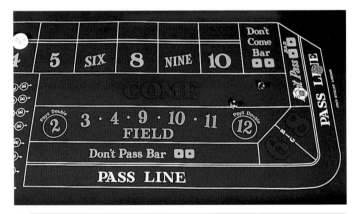

❻ Player **A** throws the dice again and scores 4. This means that a
point is established.
The puck is moved to number 4 to indicate the progress
of the game.

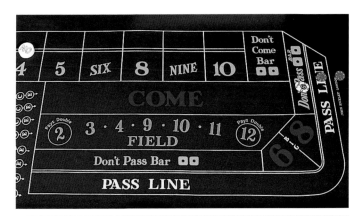

7 Player **A** makes an odds bet by placing a second chip (blue) directly behind the chip already on the pass line.

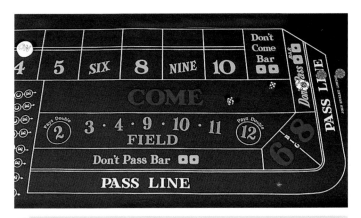

8 Player **A** continues to throw the dice, scoring 10, 5, 6, 2 and 8 consecutively. None of these throws has any effect on the bets of either player **A** or player **B**.

9 Player **A** throws again and scores a 4.
The point is now made.
Player **A**'s bet on the pass line wins and is paid at evens.

10 Player **A**'s odds bet also wins.
The odds bet is paid out at 2 to 1.

🄫 Player **A** is still the shooter and places a new bet, indicated by the blue chip, on the pass line.
The puck shows that it is still the come out roll.

🄬 Player **B** places a new bet (white chip) on the don't pass line.

TESTING A SHOOTER'S WIT

83

Playing Craps

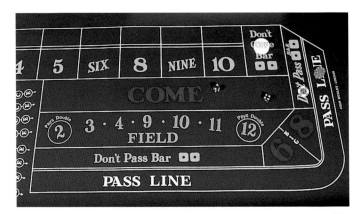

⓭ Player **A** throws the dice and scores 6.
Another point has been established.

⓮ The puck is moved to six.
Player **A** throws the dice again and scores 7.
This is a losing score.

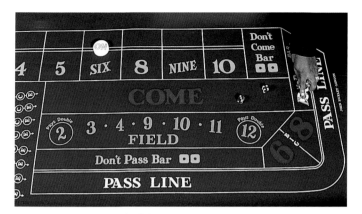

⓯ Player **A**'s bet on the pass line loses and is cleared away by the dealer. Player **B**'s bet on the don't pass line wins and is paid at evens. Because player **A** has thrown a losing score, the dice are passed to a new shooter (the player to the left of player **A**).

RIGHT *Gaming dice are precision-made cubes with squared-off corners. They are transparent to prevent them being 'loaded' (weighted to ensure they always fall on one side).*

TWO-UP

Two-up is a coin-tossing game unique to Australian casinos. It is lively and noisy with players shouting and cheering as they bet on the way the coins will fall.

The game is played in either a ring or a pit, with all the players standing around the outside of this enclosure. Inside the ring is a betting layout marked with heads, tails and odds. Bets are placed in the box marked with the desired outcome.

The game uses two coins (traditionally old pennies which are supplied by the casino). The heads side is highly polished and tails is marked with a white cross. A short piece of wood (called a kip) is used to toss the coins. Players take turns to be the spinner (the person who throws the coins).

The first spinner is the person standing to the left of the entrance to the pit (the gate). When the dealer, who is often called the boxer, announces 'come in, spinner', the spinner walks to the middle of the ring and clearly states whether he or she is going for heads or tails.

The spinner and the other players bet on whether two heads or two tails will be thrown. When all bets have been placed, the coins are thrown into the air and must reach at least 1m (3ft) above the spinner's head. The dealer ensures that the throw is valid.

One head and one tail is called odds and is a tie, resulting in all bets being frozen. Winning bets are paid at evens. For the spinner to win, three heads or three tails must be thrown consecutively. This pays the player 7.5 to 1. Players lose if five consecutive odds are thrown. This gives a house advantage of 3.12 percent. There is a 25 per cent chance that two heads or two tails will be thrown and a 50 per cent chance for one head and one tail to be thrown.

TOP *In the game Two-up, the coins have to be thrown at least 1m (3ft) above the spinner's head, otherwise a no-throw is called and all bets are frozen.*

SIC BO

Sic bo is also well-known by casino patrons as Hi-lo. Its name translates literally as 'dice pair' and its origins are an ancient Chinese gambling game played with a plate and overturned bowl. Dice would be placed between the plate and bowl and vigorously shaken. Players would bet on all the possible combinations of numbers that could be thrown. Today, three dice are shaken in a cup, which is subsequently placed bottom-up on the table with the dice hidden under it. The dealer then lifts the cup revealing the correct dice-combinations. This new structure of Sic bo is popular in Asian casinos, but is, in comparison, a relatively new addition to the modern casinos of Las Vegas and Atlantic City.

How to play the game

▶ The game is played on a table with sections of it that light up depending on the bet that wins.

▶ The betting layout is divided into four rows. The bottom row is marked with single-number bets. The next row is marked with two-number bets. The following row has the bets on the total of the three dice. The top row has 'big',

'small', triple and double bets. The payout odds for each bet are on the layout.

▶ A dealer runs the game, shakes the dice and pays out winning bets. Three dice are used and they are placed in an automatic shaking device. The dice may also be thrown manually from a cup. The winning numbers are those uppermost on the dice.

▶ Players bet on the prospective numbers or combination of numbers to be thrown. Bets can be made on individual numbers, pairs, triples (three of a kind) or combinations of any two or three of the dice. The house advantage varies between 2.78 and 33.33%. Some casinos offer better odds than others.

▶ The dealer will announce 'place your bets'. Players place their bets on the box marked with the desired outcome. For example, if you want to bet on 'big', you place your chip on the bet marked 'big'. The dealer will announce 'no more bets' and the dice are shaken.

▶ The dealer announces the winning numbers and enters them into the computer. The winning boxes on the layout light up. The dealer pays out the winning bets and removes the losing bets. New bets may not be placed until the dealer has switched off the lights.

Types of bets

There are seven different types of bets in Sic bo.

Single-number bets

▶ An individual number

This bet wins if the number selected comes up on any of the dice. Any of the numbers from one to six can be played. For example, a bet on the number five will win if a 5 comes up on any die. If two or three 5s are thrown, the payout odds are even greater. However, if no 5 is thrown, the bet loses.

Two-number bets

▶ Double

This is a bet on two numbers. For example, a bet on four and five will win if 4 comes up on one die and 5 on another. The range of possible number combinations are marked on the betting layout.

▶ Totals

The winning numbers on all three dice are added to calculate the total. For example, if 5, 4 and 2 are thrown the total will be 11. Bets made on 11 would win and all other bets on the total would lose. Any total from 4 to 17 can be played. The scores 3 and 18 cannot be made as a total bet. If the score is 3 or 18 all bets on the total lose.

▶ 'Small' or 'big'

A bet on 'small' wins if the total of the dice is between 4 and 10. For example, if 3, 5 and 1 are thrown, the total is 9 which would be a winning bet. A bet on 'big' wins if the total is between 11 and 17. For example, if 6, 4 and 3 are thrown, the total is 13 which would be a winning number. Bets on 'small' or 'big' lose if a triple is thrown.

▶ Any triple

Any triple is a bet on any three of a kind.

▶ Triple of a particular number

A particular triple is a triple made with one particular number. For example, if a triple of three 5s is played, the bet will lose if three 4s are thrown.

▶ Any pair

A win if the same number appears on any two dice, such as a throw of 4, 4, 6.

Single-number bets
An individual number
The odds paid depend on how many dice the selected number appears on. If the number comes up on one die, odds of evens are paid. If the number comes up on two dice, odds of 2/1 are paid. If the number comes up on all three dice, odds of 3/1 are paid.

Two-number bets
Double
Odds paid are 5/1.

Totals
Odds paid range from 6/1 to 60/1 depending on the total bet.

'Small' or 'big'
Odds paid on 'Small' are 1/1 and on 'big' 1/1.

Triple of a particular number
Odds paid are 150/1.

Any triple
Odds paid are 24/1 and 30/1.

Any pair
Odds paid are 8/1 and 10/1.

Single-number bets
An individual number
The house advantage is 7.87%.

Two-number bets
Double
The house advantage is 16.67%.

Totals
The house advantage depends on the number played and on the payout odds, which vary in different casinos.

'Small' or 'big'
The house advantage is 2.78%.

Triple of a particular number
The house advantage is 30.09%. At odds of 180/1 the house advantage is 16.2%.

Any triple
For odds of 24/1, the house advantage is 30.56%. For odds of 30/1 the house advantage is 13.89%.

Any pair
For odds of 8/1 the house advantage is 33.33%. For odds of 10/1 the house advantage is 18.52%

The best bet to make is a 'big' or 'small' bet, a 'big' bet being where the three dice total between 11 and 17 and a 'small' bet being a total between 4 and 10. These have the lowest house advantage.

TESTING A SHOOTER'S WIT

The High Stakes Card Game

Baccara is the highest staking of all casino games. It originated in Italy during the Middle Ages, before migrating to France where it was popular with the aristocracy. It is the game played by James Bond and real-life legends, sometimes in public but more often in the secluded confines of the *salon privé*. Baccara is particularly popular with high rollers, who often play games with no stake limit. It is not unusual for millions of dollars to be won or lost on the turn of a card. Nowadays baccara is found in Europe's exclusive casinos, such as Baden Baden and Monte Carlo.

Baccarat (with a silent 't'), also known as punto banco, is a simplified version of baccara which originated in the UK. The name used depends on where the game is played. Punto banco is the British term and baccarat tends to be used in the USA.

BACCARA

• Baccara, the forerunner of baccarat and punto banco, is played mostly in European casinos. It is particularly popular in both France and Germany. High minimum stakes are the norm in baccara and it is not at all unusual to find games with a minimum stake of US$100. Some games even start as high as US$1000 minimum.

The large baccara tables, which can accommodate up to 14 players at one time, are often located in a separate room in the casino, with entry to the highest staking games closed to all but the participants. The players and the casino dealer are seated at the table, but if there are more than 14 players the others may stand. Each playing position is marked with a number.

• Six decks of playing cards are used. Because of the size of the table, the dealer uses a large paddle to move the cards and chips around. The game is played with 'community hands'. No matter how many players there are, only two hands are dealt. One player, acting as the banker, receives one hand and the remaining players bet on the other hand.

• In most games, the house (the casino) acts as the banker and is responsible for

paying out winnings and collecting losing bets. In baccara however, the players take turns to act as the banker.

• The player whose turn it is to be the banker stakes an amount of money that will be used to pay out winning bets, which are paid at odds of evens. Losing bets are collected by the dealer and paid to the banker. The casino deducts a five per cent commission from the losing bets. The banker is also responsible for dealing the cards.

• The casino dealer controls the game, pays out the winning bets from the banker's stake, collects the losing bets from the other players on the banker's behalf, and shuffles the cards. He may also be consulted for advice.

TOP *Up to 14 players can be seated at a punto banco table at any given time.*

SCORING

Cards from two to nine inclusive have their face value. Aces count as one. Tens and the court cards (kings, queens and jacks) all have a value of 0 (zero). Two cards are dealt to the player and two to the banker. The value of the cards is added together to give the score.

If the score adds up to 10, the total becomes zero. If the total exceeds 10, then the score is the last digit, so a total of 14 becomes a score of four. The lowest possible score is zero and the highest nine. The winning hand is the one with the total closest to nine.

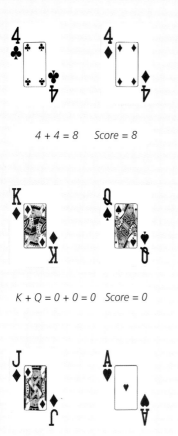

$4 + 4 = 8$ Score = 8

$K + Q = 0 + 0 = 0$ Score = 0

$J + A = 0 + 1$ Score = 1

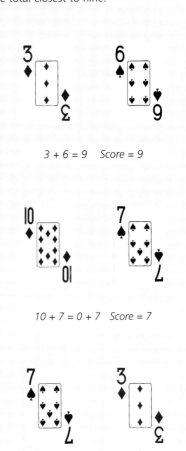

$3 + 6 = 9$ Score = 9

$10 + 7 = 0 + 7$ Score = 7

$7 + 3 = 10$
Score is the last digit = 0

PLAYING THE GAME

The object of baccara is to use a minimum of two and a maximum of three cards to try to make a score as close as possible to nine. The highest score is nine and the lowest is zero. Players aim to beat the banker's hand. After the dealer has shuffled the cards, a player cuts them by placing a blank card into the pack. A second blank card is inserted about 15 cards from the end before the cards are placed in the shoe and passed to the banker, who deals. When the blank card is reached the shoe is returned to the dealer for the cards to be reshuffled.

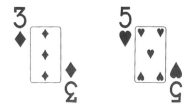

A score of eight or nine is called a natural.

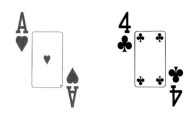

Baccara is a score between zero and five.

▶ To begin a game, the banker makes an initial bet, called the bank (*banque* or banco). This bet can be any amount over the minimum table limit and there is no upper limit to the amount that may be bet. Chips representing the bank are placed in front of the dealer.

▶ The other players (the ponte or punto) may place bets against the bank up to its total amount. Players call out what they want to bet. If a player wants to bet an amount equal to the bank, he or she calls '*banco solo*'. If more than one player calls '*banco solo*' the player closest to the banker's right has precedence (seated players take precedence over standing players). The player sitting to the immediate right of the banker is known as the prime right.

▶ A call of '*banco avec la table*' is a bet of half the bank's total and other players may only bet up to the balance of the bank. A player who loses after playing either *banco solo* or *banco avec la table* takes precedence over prime right on the next hand (*banco suivi*).

▶ Once all the bets have been placed, the banker (banco) deals four cards face down. The player (ponte) with the highest stake receives the first and third card. The banker receives the second and fourth card.

▶ After looking at the cards, the ponte makes certain plays depending on the score. With a score of zero to four, a third card is drawn (it will be dealt face up). With a score of five, taking a third card is optional.

▶ With six or seven no action is taken and the player stands. A score of eight or nine (called a natural) is immediately revealed (turned face up). Any score between zero and five is called baccara.

▶ If the player (ponte) has a score of eight or nine, the banker cannot take a third card, regardless of his score and he must stand but for any other total, the player must follow the rules for drawing a third card, according to the table below.

▶ The banker's decision about whether or not to take a third card depends on the player's action. If the banker does not have a total of eight or nine, then the same action as the player is taken.

Action to be followed by the player after the first two cards are dealt

Total score	Action to be taken
0, 1, 2, 3, 4	A third card is drawn
5	Taking a third card is optional
6, 7	No action is taken
8, 9	Hand is immediately revealed

TOP RIGHT *In baccara, when the banker wins, five per cent commission is deducted from the losing bets before the balance is paid to the banker.*

▶ If the banker has a score of five, a third card must be drawn. If the player has drawn a third card, then the banker's decision depends on his score and the value of the player's third card.

▶ If the ponte mistakenly draws a card when the rules say he should stand, the value is added to his hand, which can result in a winning hand losing.

▶ In some casinos neither the banker, nor a player who has bet an equal amount (*banco solo*), are obliged to follow the rules about drawing cards and have more freedom to choose their course of action.

▶ A player who accepts the bank must pay its full value. If no player accepts the bank it is offered to the highest bidder.

Banker's action after player draws third card		
Banker's score	Player's third card	Banker's action
3	8	stands
3	Anything other than 8	draws
4	2, 3, 4, 5, 6, 7	draws
4	0, 1, 8, 9	stands
5	0, 1, 2, 3, 8, 9	stands
5	4, 5, 6, 7	draws
6	0, 1, 2, 3, 4 ,5, 8, 9	stands
6	6, 7	draws
7	0, 1, 2, 3, 4, 5, 8, 9	stands
8, 9	Player cannot draw	stands

▶ The winner is the player with the highest score up to nine. If the ponte's score ties with the banker's, the hand is replayed. When the ponte wins, the bets are paid out from the bank at evens. When the banker wins, the dealer collects the losing bets from the pontes, deducts five per cent commission and then adds the remainder to the bank.

If the banker wins, he or she may choose to keep the bank or pass it to the right instead. Should the banker lose the bank, it automatically passes to the right, but players are not obliged to accept it. It is worth keeping the bank if you have it, however, as the house advantage (or house edge – the percentage of the stake retained by the casino as profit) for the bank is much lower, at 1.06 per cent, than the house edge for the players, which is 1.23 per cent.

LEFT *In the 1965 film* Thunderball *Sean Connery, as James Bond, is inscrutable as he ponders a critical decision at the baccarat table.*

PAYOUT ODDS

The payout odds are different for players' and the banker's bets.

The payout odds on winning players' bets is evens or 1/1. This means for every $1 that wins, $1 will be paid out. For example, if a player bets $100 and wins, the winning bet of $100 will be paid $100 by the banker. The player also retains the stake giving a total of $200. The nett effect is that the player wins $100, the banker loses $100 and the casino gets nothing.

> **$100 on a stake of $100**

If the bank wins, odds of evens (less 5 per cent commission) is paid, which equates to odds of 19/20. This means that for a $1 bet $0.95 will be paid out: one dollar less five cents commission ($1 – $0.05).

If a player stakes $100, the banker also stakes $100 against the bet. If the banker wins, the banker will be paid the $100 that the player has staked, less 5% commission of $5, giving a total of $95. The banker also retains its own stake, giving a total of $195. The commission is paid to the casino. The nett effect is that the banker wins $95, the player loses $100 and the casino gets $5.

> **$95 on a stake of $100**

HOUSE ADVANTAGE

The house advantage on baccara is different on the banker's and players' bets, as it is with the payout odds. The house advantage is 1.06% on the banker's bets and 1.23% on the players'. Mathematically the banker will win 45.84% of the hands and the players will win 44.61% of the time. The other 9.55% of bets will be tied.

If, for example, $100 is bet, the banker will win $45.84 less 5% commission of $2.29 and will lose $44.61 to the player. This gives a nett loss of $1.06 which goes to the casino. This means the house advantage on the banker's bets is 1.06 per cent. The player will win $44.61 and lose $45.84 giving a loss of 1.23 per cent. This means the house advantage on the player's bets will be 1.23 per cent.

The house advantage for baccara is less than that for all the other table games, making it the best value-for-money game in the casino. However, the disadvantage is that there is no real strategy that can be used to affect the outcome of the game. Unlike other card games, card counting does not help. There is no particular skill involved in playing and players are simply reliant on luck. Betting on baccara is similar to betting on the toss of a coin.

BACCARAT & PUNTO BANCO

• Baccarat as well as Midi and Mini Punto Banco are played on smaller tables and are dealt at a faster speed than baccara. Minimum stakes are around $5, which is less than the high stakes normally played for at traditional baccara tables.

• Baccarat and Punto Banco differ from baccara in that the casino acts as the banker, paying out winnings and collecting losing bets. In American casinos, baccarat players take turns to act as the dealer, but in punto banco that role is fulfilled by the casino.

• Between four and eight decks of cards are used and the game is still played with community cards (all the players bet on the same hand). The rules on scoring and drawing cards are the same as for baccara.

• Players have three choices when betting. They can bet on the banker (the casino), on the player, or on a tie between the two.

• To begin the game, the dealer shuffles the cards and invites a player to cut them by placing a blank card into the pack. The dealer places the cards in the shoe (*sabot*) and inserts a blank card

about one deck from the end to indicate when the cards will be reshuffled.

• After each player has made his or her bet, four cards are dealt face down by the dealer. The cards for the player's hand are placed in the area of the table marked 'Punto' or 'Player'. The player looks at the cards and draws additional cards according to the rules.

• When the player's score is determined, the banker's hand is dealt with according to the rules. In the case of a tie, neither the bets on the player (punto) nor the banker (banco) lose, and bets on the tie are paid out. Winning bets on the player are paid at evens. Winning bets on the banker are also paid at evens, less 5 per cent commission, which works out at odds of 19 to 20.

BACCARAT

PAYOUT ODDS

The player's bet is paid at odds of evens (1/1).

The banker's bet is paid at odds of evens less 5% commission or at odds of 19/20.

The odds on a tie-bet vary from 8/1 to 9/1 depending on where the game is played.

HOUSE ADVANTAGE

The house advantage is 1.06 if the bank wins. If punto wins, the house advantage is 1.24%. For a tie, the house advantage is 14.4%.

MIDI PUNTO BANCO

PAYOUT ODDS

On the smaller tables there are games where the odds are paid out similarly to the traditional games. Winning players' bets are paid out at evens and winning banker's bets are paid out at evens less 5% which works out at odds of 19/20.

Another version of the game, Punto Banco 2000, simplifies the payout odds. Most British casinos now offer Punto Banco 2000 in place of the traditional game. Punto Banco 2000 eliminates the need for calculating the 5% commission as in the traditional game. All bets are paid at evens except when the bank wins with a score of 6. Then odds of 1/2 are paid. For a tie, odds of 8/1 are paid. All the other rules regarding the dealing of the cards are exactly the same as those of the traditional game. The faster calculation of the payout helps to speed up the playing of the game.

HOUSE ADVANTAGE

As the odds on Punto Banco 2000 differ greatly from those of the traditional games, the house advantage is different. On banco bets the house advantage is 1.45% compared to 1.06% in the traditional game. On punto bets it is 1.23% and for a tie it is 14.4%. It is thus more profitable to bet on punto on the smaller tables.

OPPOSITE *Mini and midi punto banco tables are the size of blackjack tables.*

❶ Most casinos offer punto banco on mini or midi tables, as the games are simpler to operate and easier to play. The difference between them is the number of players they can accommodate.

❷ The game begins with the players making their bets.
Player **A** (on the left) bets five chips on player (punto).
Player **B** bets five chips on banker (banco).
Player **C** bets five chips on a tie.

3 Two cards are dealt face up to each hand.
The player (punto) is dealt 5 and 3 which is a score of eight.
The bank (banco) is dealt 10 and 8. As 10 counts for 0 (zero), this
is also a score of eight, which means there is a tie.

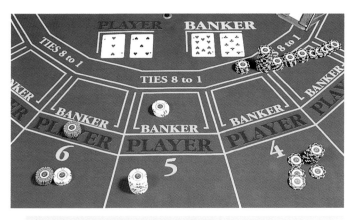

4 Player C's bet on a tie is paid out at 8 to 1.
The cards are cleared away and the game continues.

5 Player **A** bets on the player again, and player **B** on the banker.
Player **C** does not bet this time.
Two new hands are dealt.
The ponte receives 9 and 4 – a score of three (9 + 4 = 13 = 3)
which means a third card must be drawn.

6 Another card is dealt to the player.
It is a 10 and as this counts as zero the score remains three.
The banker received 4 + 10 which totals four (0 + 4 = 4).
The banker has the highest score up to nine so wins the hand.

7 The banker wins and the bet is paid at evens.

8 The player's bet loses and the stake is removed.

The Luck of the Draw

Poker conjures up images of saloons in the old West where hustlers and gun fighters did battle. It seems that no Hollywood Western is complete without a gunfight over a poker game, but this way of life was often the reality for professional gamblers in the Wild West. In 1876 a famous lawman, James Butler 'Wild Bill' Hickok, lost his life in a poker game in Deadwood, South Dakota. To this day his last hand – a pair of aces over eights – is known as the 'dead man's hand'.

Nowadays playing poker is not so risky. Players may lose their stake but at least they stay alive. Variations on the game, with their own rules, have been well adapted for casinos.

POKER

Poker, a card game played by two to 10 players, is based on the ranking of the hands. The game is played with one standard deck of 52 playing cards. Players aim to win the pot by having the highest-ranking five-card hand. When poker is played in a casino, a dealer is provided and the casino charges the players either an hourly rate or a percentage of the pot (called the rake – typically between five and 10 per cent of the pot). There are many variations of poker. Each has different rules about the total number of cards dealt and the specific method of betting, but they all have in common the ranking of the hands and the action that must be taken.

Types of poker played in casinos include five-card draw, seven-card stud, Texas hold 'em and Omaha. Caribbean poker (also known as casino poker) differs from the other versions in that players play against the casino, not against each other. Games of the same name may be played differently in some casinos, so it is important to check the rules before playing.

BELOW *Playing poker can be entertaining and fun, and the thrill of a win enhances even a social game of poker.*

The basic action that takes place in a poker game can be summarized as follows:

Raise: a bet that players must either match or exceed.

Call: to bet the same amount as the preceding player in order to remain in the game.

Fold: to withdraw from the game and lose all the money you have staked.

▶ At the beginning of each game, the pot is seeded to ensure there is at least some money on the game. Seeding is done in various ways. In some games, before play commences all the players are required to make a bet called an ante, which is usually equivalent to the minimum stake. In others, there are rounds of blind betting in which bets of varying amounts are made before the players look at their hands.

▶ Some casinos may have fixed rules about betting, such as specific amounts that stakes can be raised by or that a bet or raise must fall within a spread limit (such as any amount between $1 and $5). Players should ensure they are familiar with local systems before getting into a game.

▶ After the cards are dealt the players can discard and exchange them before a second round of betting takes place. Betting moves clockwise until each player has either called all bets or folded. A showdown then takes place with each player still in the game revealing their cards. The last player to bet is the first to show his or her hand, with the other hands revealed in turn.

▶ Players with losing hands may discard their cards without the other players seeing them and they will lose their stakes. The player with the highest-ranking hand wins the pot. In a tie, the pot is split equally.

RANKING OF THE HANDS

A poker hand usually consists of five cards. Aces are the highest ranked cards, followed by kings, queens and jacks, then the numbers in descending order with 2s being the lowest. The suits do not affect the rankings. The photographs below show the order in which the hands are ranked.

Royal flush – *the best hand, comprising ace, king, queen, jack and 10 of the same suit.*

Straight flush – *five cards of the same suit in consecutive numerical order.*

Four of a kind – *four cards of the same value with any other card.*

Full house – *three cards of the same value (three of a kind) plus a pair (two cards of the same value).*
Where two players have a full house the hand with the highest value for the three of a kind wins.

Flush – five cards of the same suit in any numerical order. If two players have this hand, the one with a higher value wins.

Straight – any five cards in numerical order. A, K, Q, J, 10 is the highest, or top straight, followed by K, Q, J, 10, 9.

Three of a kind – three cards of the same value and two others. For two players with the same hand see 'Flush'.

Two pairs – two pairs with another card. For players with the same pair, the other card's ranking decides who wins.

One pair – two cards of the same value with three cards of different values. For players with the same pair see 'Flush'.

Highest card – if none of the above hands are held, the winner is the player with the highest card.

JOINING A GAME

On entering a card room there will most probably be a number of games in progress as well as players waiting. New players need to register to get into a game. The player's name will be placed on a list and he or she will be called as soon as a seat is free at a table. Casino staff will direct players to the appropriate table when their name is called.

Players are not usually allowed to buy chips during the course of a game so sufficient chips should be purchased beforehand to last for an entire game. All chips must remain on the table throughout the game.

Although the minimum stakes for poker may appear low, a game like Five-Card Draw needs chips to the value of about 40 times the minimum stake. Seven-card stud requires about 50 times, while Hold 'em and Omaha need around 100 times the minimum stake. If a player runs out of money (chips) during a game, a second pot will be played for. The player who has no further funds still has a chance to win the first pot, while the other players continue to play for both pots.

TABLE ETIQUETTE

▶ Players are only allowed to touch their own cards and chips. Everything else on the table is out of bounds. Their particular cards must always remain in view (players are not allowed to put cards into a pocket, for example).

▶ Take care when handling your cards. If another player sees them, your hand may be declared dead and you can take no further part in that game. Dropping cards also results in the hand being declared dead.

▶ Do not throw chips at the pot or at the dealer. Bets are made by placing chips directly in front of you. The dealer will check you have bet the correct amount and will put the chips into the pot. It is important to give clear verbal instructions of your action. Call for 'time' if you need to make a decision. Players still in a game show this by placing a chip on top of their cards.

▶ The dealer is responsible for dealing the cards, removing losing hands, exchanging money for chips, giving change for large denomination chips and paying the pot to the winner, who normally tips the dealer.

▶ Players may leave the card table for a short break, during which the dealer will watch your chips. Some rooms specify a time limit for breaks and may allocate the seat to another player if you are gone for too long.

STRATEGY

Chances of making a ranking hand
Using a standard deck of 52 cards there are 2,598,960 possible five-card hands that can be dealt. The table below shows the chances and odds of making each ranked hand.

HAND	NUMBER OF WAYS IT CAN BE MADE WITH FIVE CARDS	ODDS OF MAKING A RANKING HAND FROM THE FIRST FIVE CARDS DEALT
Royal flush	4	649,739 to 1
Straight flush	36	72,192 to 1
Four of a kind	624	4,164 to 1
Full house	3,744	693 to 1
Flush	5,108	508 to 1
Straight	10,200	254 to 1
Three of a kind	54,912	46 to 1
Two pairs	123,552	20 to 1
One pair	1,908,240	1,5 to 1
Highest card	1,302,540	1 to 1

HOUSE ADVANTAGE

The house advantage on poker is five per cent. With most other casino games, the house advantage is built into the payout odds. Since there are no set payout odds with most of the poker games, the casino takes a percentage of the pot. The house advantage is whatever the casino deducts from the pot. This is commonly 5 per cent but can be as high as 10 per cent. If, for example, the pot contains $100, the casino will take $5.

PAYOUT ODDS

In poker the payout is the amount of the pot less the casino's percentage, which you will not know in advance. The payout odds will vary as the game continues depending on how much money has been contributed to the pot. The ante bets ensure there is at least some money in the pot to start. The odds increase with more players. For example, if there are four players only and each of them contributes $10 to the pot, for your $10 dollar bet you have the chance to win $40. This works out at odds of 3/1. The casino also takes 5 per cent of the pot which cuts your winnings to $38. This works out at odds of 2.8/1. If, in the case of Caribbean Stud Poker, you play with seven players and each of them contributes $10, the odds are 6/1. For your $10 bet you have the chance to win $70. After the 5% is paid to the casino, you are left with $66.50. This works out at odds of 5.65/1.

KEY ELEMENTS TO WINNING

▶ There are several main elements to a poker game. These include getting the best hand, understanding the mathematics of poker, winning the highest possible jackpot, managing your money and outwitting the other players.

▶ One of the crucial factors in poker is understanding the value of your hand. You need to quickly decide whether or not your hand is worth playing and to appreciate the chances the other players have of beating your hand. If you study the chart showing the chances of making a ranking hand, (see p108–109) you will see that the chances of making the highest ranking hands are small. You need to get a feel for what is a good hand and worth playing. You can practise this at home by dealing out dummy hands for yourself and other players. When you see your hand, make a decision about whether to play or fold. Then take a look at the other players' hands to discover whether or not you made a good decision. Continue to do this until you are confident that you are able to select hands with a good chance of winning.

▶ If you decide your hand is not worth playing, you need to withdraw from the game as early as possible. Staying in for an extra round of betting will cost you a lot of money over time.

▶ If you have a good hand, you need to try to maximize your winnings by getting as many players as possible to contribute to the pot. If you bet too high at the beginning of the game, you frighten other players into folding which leads to a smaller pot. A bet at the right level will help to encourage other players to continue betting. Small raises will more likely keep them in the game. If you have a poor hand and intend to bluff, once the pot has reached a sufficient level you need to bet aggressively to force the other players into folding.

▶ It helps to develop a style of playing that is varied so that other players cannot immediately spot whether you have a good hand. Controlling your body language also helps you to become a better player. Your facial expressions, mannerisms, tone of voice and fidgeting can be interpreted by the other players to work out whether or not you have a good hand. If, for example, you get a fantastic hand, you may be tempted to look at it again and again because it is so unbelievable. Alternatively, you may nonchalantly throw chips into the pot or always fiddle with your chips. You can be sure the other players will also notice when you do not have confidence in your hand as you are likely to be indecisive and take too long to play.

KEY ELEMENTS TO WINNING

▶ Being able to spot when a player is bluffing is extremely helpful. By observing a player's usual movements and watching for subtle changes in them you can learn to detect players who are bluffing. There are lots of physical signs that you can look out for that show a person is lying. These include wandering eyes, fidgeting, a change in tone of voice, shifting back and forth, sweating, shaking, covering the eyes, mouth or nose, licking the lips, running the tongue over the teeth, and leaning forward. If you suspect that someone is bluffing, a direct question to them about their hand can help to confirm your suspicions. Ask directly "do you have a good hand?" and watch the reaction. Staring at players can be intimidating for some. Other players will be good at suppressing their mannerisms and expressions. A player who suddenly appears to be sitting very still when they were previously relaxed and freely moving may also be bluffing.

▶ If you want to pull off a bluff, keep an expressionless face, look your opponents in the eye and sit still without fidgeting. This will make it difficult for them to work out whether or not you are bluffing. When you look at your cards, do so just once and memorize them. It is also possible to use false body language to confuse players. However, be subtle.

▶ With some players it will be easy to work out whether or not they have good hands. Some players never bluff and will only play good hands.

▶ When you make a bet you will need to consider your chances of winning with your hand compared to the chances the other players have of beating you. Your knowledge of the players will also help you decide if any are bluffing. With a large pot, for example, the temptation to try to pull off a bluff is greater. In contrast, players are less likely to compete for a smaller pot. On the other hand, lots of small wins soon mount up.

▶ Ensure you have enough money to see you through to the end of a game. If you run out of money with a good hand, you will not get a share of the second pot that could grow significantly towards the end of a game.

▶ If you hit a losing streak, stay calm. There may be a strong temptation to try to get back your losses. Don't try to recoup them by making big bets or even attempt to continue betting because you have contributed a lot to the pot. Also, don't try to play a bluff if you are very nervous. The other players will recognize your intense desperation to win and capitalize on this.

If you hold three of a kind, you can either exchange one or both cards to try to improve your hand. Exchanging two cards gives you a better chance of achieving a full house or four of a kind. If you exchange two cards, the other players have a good indication of your hand. They will know that you either have a pair with an extra card or three of a kind. Anyone with a high three of a kind can be pretty confident that they already have the edge on you. Alternatively, you could also simply exchange one card. You have less of a chance of improving your hand but in doing so you can give the impression that you are either already holding a high-ranking hand of four of a kind or that you simply need one card to complete a high hand like a flush or a full house. The possibility that you may have two pairs could be enough to make someone with one pair fold. This is because the chances of improving a two-pair to a full house are far better than improving one pair to a full house. It is also possible to exchange no cards and play the hand of three of a kind. By betting aggressively towards the end of the game it would be possible to force other players out. The action that you take will be based on your knowledge of the other players and their playing sequences.

HOW TO PLAY FIVE-CARD DRAW

Each player receives five cards face down. When all the cards have been dealt, the players look at their own cards. After an initial round of betting they have the opportunity to exchange any cards in their hand for new cards from the deck. Cards that are being discarded are returned to the dealer before the new cards are drawn.

As a general rule, if you get nothing from the initial deal you should fold (that is, if you are unable to make a ranking of at least a high pair). Only a hand with a pair of at least six or more is worth playing. The total number of cards then exchanged, gives a player an indication of the strength of his or her hand. A player holding just one pair can improve his or her hand by exchanging up to three cards. However if three cards are exchanged, the player then makes it obvious that the hand contains a pair. By exchanging only two cards some doubt remains as to whether the player holds a pair or three of a kind. The extra card retained, which is called a kicker, is usually the highest other card in the hand.

In the illustrations on the following pages, the players' cards are not revealed but are indicated to the reader in the accompanying text. Play moves clockwise around the table, with Player A in the 12-o'clock position, Player B in the 3-o'clock position and so on.

Playing Five-Card Draw

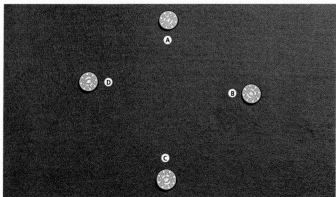

1 To start the game, the pot is seeded.
This means that each player makes a bet of equal value.

2 Five cards are dealt face down to each player.

Player **A** holds:	3♦	10♦	4♠	8♠	5♣
Player **B** holds:	9♥	9♣	10♥	K♦	2♠
Player **C** holds:	4♥	5♥	6♣	10♠	K♣
Player **D** holds:	Q♠	Q♦	3♠	4♦	A♣

Playing Five-Card Draw

❸ Player **A** has been dealt nothing and as the chances of getting one pair from exchanging three cards are slim, player **A** folds.

All the money contributed by player **A** to the pot is lost.

❹ Player **B** has a high pair, which is worth playing and takes two cards, retaining a kicker. Now the other players do not know if one pair or three of a kind are held, or if player **B** is bluffing.

Player **B**'s new cards: Q♣   2♦

Player **B** now holds: 9♥   9♣   K♦   Q♣   2♦

❺ Player **C** has nothing but has the possibility of making a straight flush, a flush or a straight. Player **C** draws two new cards.

Player **D** has a pair of queens (a high pair) and decides to take two cards, retaining one card as a kicker.

Player **C**'s new cards: 6♠   7♥
Player **D**'s new cards: 8♥   7♣
Player **C** now holds: 4♥   5♥   6♣   6♠   7♥
Player **D** now holds: Q♦   Q♠   8♥   7♣   A♣

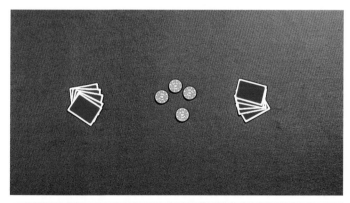

❻ Player **B**'s hand is not improved after the draw but he stays in the game.

Player **C** now has a low pair and folds.

Player **D**'s hand is not improved but he also stays in the game.

Playing Five-Card Draw

7 It has now become a test of nerve between players **B** and **D** and they continue to bet.
Player **B** has the confidence to keep raising his bets.

8 The pot gradually increases as betting continues.

❾ Player **B** has sufficient confidence in his hand to continue to raise. Player **D** initially decides to match player **B** but eventually he loses his nerve and folds.

❿ Player **B** is therefore the winner and keeps the pot.
As player **D** has folded player **B** does not have to reveal his cards. In fact, player **D**'s hand was worth more than player **B**'s hand, but player **B** managed to force player **D** out of the game.

HOW TO PLAY FIVE-CARD STUD

▶ Stud poker differs from draw poker in that some of the cards in each player's hand are revealed to the other players. The object of both games remains the same, that is, to beat the other players' hands by making the best ranking poker hand.

▶ To begin, each player receives one card face up and one card face down. A player with the lowest face-up card makes an initial bet, called a forced bet, in order to get the betting started. The remaining three cards are then dealt face up to each player, with a round of betting taking place after each card is dealt. The player showing the highest ranking hand is the first to bet in each remaining round.

▶ As five-card stud progresses, each player gets more information about the other players' hands on which to base his or her subsequent bets. A good initial hand is one that matches or betters the highest card showing on the table at that time. Anything lower and you should consider folding.

RATING THE COMPETITION

You need to compare your hand with what is revealed by the other players' hands. From this you will be aware of the various possible hands other players can have. See the illustrations on the following pages for an example.

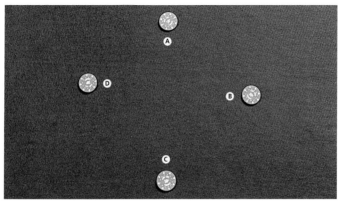

1 Players begin the game by seeding the pot.

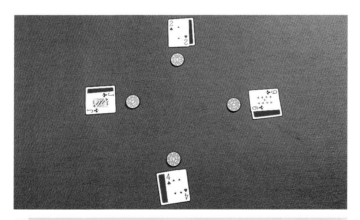

2 Two cards are dealt to each player, one face up and the other face down. The players look at their face-down card.
Player A has nothing of value.
Player B has a pair of 9s – an initial hand worth playing.
Players C and D have a Jack each, which is also worth playing.
Player A's down card: 5♣ Player B's down card: 9♠
Player C's down card: J♦ Player D's down card: 7♥

Playing Five-Card Stud

③ Player **A** must bet first as he is showing the lowest face-up card.

④ To stay in the game, each player makes a bet equal to player **A**'s bet.

⑤ The next round of cards is dealt.
Player **A**'s new card: 8♦
Player **B**'s new card: A♦
Player **C**'s new card: 4♦
Player **D**'s new card: 7♣

⑥ Player **B** is showing the highest-ranking hand (with an ace as the high card) and must bet first.
Players **C** and **D** call (they make a bet equal to player **B**'s bet).

7 Player **A** folds.
His cards are returned to the dealer and he loses his stake.

8 The next card is dealt.
Player **B**'s new card: 4♥
Player **C**'s new card: 3♥
Player **D**'s new card: 3♣

9 Player **C** is now showing the highest-ranking hand with a pair of 4s, so bets first.

10 Player **C** raises. Players **B** and **D** call.
The next card is then dealt.
Player **B**'s new card: A♣
Player **C**'s new card: J♠
Player **D**'s new card: 7♦

⓫ Player **B** has two pairs (aces over 9s) and knows he has beaten player **C**'s hand unless player **C** has three of a kind with fours.

The fact that player **B** has a 4 in his hand makes it less likely that **C** has three of a kind.

Player **B** can also see that if player **D** has two pairs, he has beaten him. However, he knows that if player **D** has three of a kind with 7s then player **D** will win.

Player **C** has two pairs (Jacks over 4s). Player **C** can see that **B** has a possible two pairs which would beat his two pairs and that **D** has a possible three of a kind which would also beat his hand.

Player **D** has three of a kind with 7s. He knows that player **B** can only beat him if his hole (down) card is an ace. **D** knows he has beaten player **C**'s best possible hand of three of a kind (with 4s).

As player **B** is showing the highest-ranking hand, with a pair of aces, he bets first.

It is important to decide early on if your hand is worth playing. The decision to play or fold should be made after the first three cards have been dealt. If you have nothing worth playing after the first three cards, you should fold. Continually staying in the betting and hoping your last four cards will be good ones is costly. Good hands to play are three of a kind or a high pair.

12 Player **B** raises again.
Player **C** realizes he cannot match the other players and folds.
His cards are removed by the dealer and he loses his stake.

13 Player **D** meets player **B**'s challenge and raises.
In response, player **B** raises again.

⑭ Player **D** raises. (Each raise bet must be met or exceeded by the next player if he or she wants to remain in the game.)

⑮ Player **B** calls (bets the same amount as player **D**'s last bet).

16 Player **D** raises.
Player **B** loses his nerve and is now convinced that player **D** must have three of a kind, so he folds.

17 Player **D** wins the pot.
Player **D** holds: 7♥ 7♣ 7♦ J♣ 3♣
His winning cards were three of a kind: 7♥ 7♣ 7♦

ASSESSING YOUR HAND

▶ Three of a kind is the best hand that you can initially get and is worth playing. Look at what the other players have and assess if any of them can beat you. Suppose you have three kings and two other players have an ace showing, their chances of improving are less than yours. One player may have three aces which would beat your hand, but since the other ace is in another player's hand, there is no chance of getting four aces. If no other kings are showing, there is the possibility of you getting four kings. Four kings would beat three aces. It would also beat a full house.

▶ A high pair is a good hand. Check that your chances of improving are not limited because your desired cards are held by other players. If you hold a low pair, assess your chances against what you can glean from the other hands.

▶ If you have three cards to a possible flush or straight, make sure none of your desired cards are in the other players' hands. Bear in mind that an open-ended flush or straight is easier to achieve than a closed one. For example, Q, J, 10, 9, will be easier to complete than A, K, Q, J, as it could be completed with a king or an 8 (eight possible cards), whereas the latter can only be completed by a 10 (four possible cards).

HOW TO PLAY SEVEN-CARD STUD

▶ Each player receives a total of seven cards and the aim is to make the best-possible hand from those cards. Three cards are initially dealt (two face down and one face up). The player with the lowest up card makes a forced bet. A button (marker) then travels around the table to clearly indicate which player is to make the forced bet in the next game.

▶ After the forced bet each player may fold, call or raise when it is their turn. The fourth, fifth and sixth cards are dealt face up and the seventh face down. After each card is dealt there is a round of betting. The player with the highest-ranking hand on view is the first to either bet or fold in each round of betting.

▶ After all seven cards have been dealt, four cards are on display to the other players and three are hidden from view. With each round of betting, players obtain more information on which to base their strategy, enabling a player to deduce what chance his or her cards have of winning.

▶ If a player's cards have the potential to make a good hand, he or she has the option of bluffing, even if there is nothing of value in their hidden cards. By continually raising the stakes, it is possible to force the other players into folding, in which case the player's bluff will have been called.

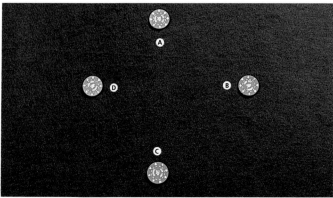

1 The aim of seven-card stud is to make the best-possible five-card poker hand from the seven cards dealt.
To begin playing, the pot is seeded.

2 Each player receives three cards (two face down and one face up).
Player **C** has the lowest up card so makes a forced bet.
Player **A** down: 10♥ 10♠   Player **B** down: Q♥ Q♦
Player **C** down: 10♦ 4♥   Player **D** down: 6♣ 6♦

❸ After the forced bet each player in turn may fold, call or raise. The fourth, fifth and sixth cards are dealt face up and the seventh is dealt face down.

Player **A** has a pair of 10s in his hole (down) cards.

Player **B** has a pair of queens in his hole cards.

Player **C** has nothing.

Player **D** has a pair of 6s.

❹ After each card is dealt there is a round of betting.

The player with the highest card on view is the first to bet or fold in each round.

When all the cards have been dealt, four cards are on display and three are hidden from view.

5 Players **A** and **B** both have two pairs (**B**'s pairs are higher).
Player **C** has a straight.
Player **D** has a full house.
On a showdown, player **D**'s hand wins.

*In the final outcome player **D** won, but in seven-card stud,
outcomes are not always predictable.*

Player **B** had a good initial hand and should have attempted to force
the other players into folding before they improved on their hands.
By pushing the betting high early on, player **D** might have been forced
to fold, as initially he only had a low pair.
Player **C** had nothing special in his hole cards and could also have been
forced out early, but by staying in he improved to a good hand.

The players up (visible) cards are:

Player **A** up:	J♦	4♦	2♦	4♠
Player **B** up:	9♦	A♦	A♠	2♥
Player **C** up:	5♦	3♠	5♥	6♥
Player **D** up:	9♦	6♠	8♥	3♦

The players down (hidden) cards are:

Player **A** down:	10♥	10♠	3♥
Player **B** down:	Q♥	Q♦	K♠
Player **C** down:	10♦	4♥	7♣
Player **D** down:	6♣	6♦	8♦

HOW TO PLAY TEXAS HOLD 'EM

● Each player receives two cards face down. Five cards are placed face up in the centre of the table. They are called community cards and are used by all the players. Each player uses a combination of the two cards in his or her hand and the five community cards to make the best possible five-card hand.

● The game begins with the players being dealt their two hole (down) cards. After they look at them a round of betting follows. The player to the left of the dealer makes an ante bet (called a small blind) and the player after him makes a second bet, normally double the value (called the big blind). The other players bet by matching at least the value of the big blind. This helps to increase the pot.

● When the first round of betting is complete, three of the community cards are dealt face up (the flop). Another round of betting follows, with the players now assessing their chances of making a winning hand from the cards they hold plus the revealed community cards. Players who feel that they have no cards of any value, will fold at this stage.

● After the next community card is dealt there is a further round of betting before the final community card (the river) is dealt, followed by more betting. The flop also gives an indication of what hands are

possible. Before the flop each player needs to decide whether or not his or her hand is worth playing. It is worth playing if the cards include any pair (not just a high pair), consecutive cards of the same suit, or fairly high cards of the same suit.

● After the flop the players have more information and can see what their possible hands might be. Occasionally, a player may be in a position where he or she knows that his or her hand is the best hand possible – called nuts.

Player **A**'s hole (hidden) cards are two aces. He stays in the game.
Player **B** has two low cards and folds.
Player **C** has a pair of 8s.
Player **D** has a king and jack of the same suit. After the turn, player **A** thinks he is in a position to have the best hand (nuts). Once all the community cards have been dealt Player **A** knows he has nuts. He needs to try to keep the betting going to increase the pot, as he knows he can't fail to win.

▶ Each player receives four cards face down (hole cards). Five community cards are placed face up in the centre of the table, to be used by all the players. Players win by making the best possible ranking hand using two of the cards in their own hand plus any three of the community cards. The game is dealt in a similar way to Hold 'em. Four cards are dealt, followed by the flop (the first three community cards). The remaining two community cards are dealt individually.

▶ After each deal there is a round of betting. Betting blind is also a possibility. After looking at their hole cards, each player decides whether or not the hand is worth playing.

▶ Unlike other versions of poker, conventional scoring is not always going to produce a winning hand. For example, four of a kind is not worth playing, as only two of the hole cards can be used, which gives a pair, and this cannot be improved upon.

▶ Three of a kind is not a good hand as there is a small chance of receiving the fourth in the community cards. The same is true of being dealt four cards that might make a flush (five cards of the same suit in any numerical order), as the chances of making a flush from the community cards are drastically reduced.

▶ In Omaha, the best possible cards to play with are a high pair or two high cards of the same suit, either of which could lead to a flush.

▶ After the flop, a player needs to, where possible, strategically force out any other player who could potentially beat his or her hand. In Omaha it is also possible for a player to have nuts – the best possible hand.

Player **A** has two high cards of the same suit. Player **B** has a king and a 10.
Player **C** has four of a kind in his hole cards. As his chances of improving are nil, he folds. Player **D** has a pair of queens. Players **A**, **B** and **D** make their bets. The flop reveals that player **A** has a straight. He knows only a higher straight can beat him. **B** has a full house and knows only a flush can beat him. Player **D** does not improve so folds. Betting continues between players **A** and **B**. If neither folds the game will go to a showdown, which player **A** will win.

THE LUCK OF THE DRAW

HOW TO PLAY CARIBBEAN STUD POKER

▶ In Caribbean stud (or casino) poker the players bet against the dealer instead of the other players. Up to seven players can play at one time. It is played on a special table and uses a single deck of 52 cards.

▶ To enter the game, players make an initial bet by placing a chip in the box marked 'ante'. The dealer deals five cards face down to each player and five cards to himself (four face down and the fifth face up). After looking at their cards the players decide whether to play or fold. If a player folds, the dealer takes the cards and the ante bet is lost.

▶ If a player decides to play, another bet (the bonus bet) of twice the ante must be made and placed in the box marked 'raise'. Wins are paid at a predetermined bonus rate for this bet (see table below).

When all the players have placed their bets, the dealer reveals his down cards. To play, the dealer must hold at least one ace or king. If the dealer qualifies, each player's hand is compared with the dealer's. If a player has a higher hand, their ante bet is paid at odds of evens and their raise (bonus) bet is paid according to the table of odds. If the player's hand ranks lower than the dealer's, both the ante and the raise bets are lost. If the dealer's hand does not qualify, the ante bet is paid at even money and the raise bet is returned.

Gaming with a difference

This game differs from other games of poker because the casino acts as the banker, paying out all winning bets and collecting losing bets. Instead of playing against each other, players bet against the casino. Individual players do not have to be concerned about what hands the other players have. They only have to concentrate on beating the dealer's hand. With this game you do not have the option of bluffing or the opportunity to force the dealer into folding by betting aggressively. You need to decide whether to fold or raise. Folding means you lose your ante bet. If you raise, you could win the ante and the raise bet should the dealer's hand qualify and your hand beats his. You could also lose the ante and the raise bet if the dealer qualifies and his hand beats yours. Pairs should always be played. You should fold if you don't have at least an ace and a king.

ODDS ON RAISE (BONUS) BET	
HAND	BONUS
Straight flush	50 to 1
Four of a kind	20 to 1
Full house	7 to 1
Flush	6 to 1
Straight	4 to 1
Three of a kind	3 to 1
Two pairs	2 to 1
One pair	even money

PAYOUT ODDS

Some casinos offer the option of an additional bet on Caribbean stud poker. This is a progressive jackpot for high-ranking hands. To qualify for this jackpot, an additional $1 bet needs to be made before the cards are dealt. A percentage of the bets made on the progressive jackpots is added to the total jackpot. Typically around 75 per cent of the bet is added to the jackpot. Each time someone bets on the jackpot the amount that can be won increases. The total value of the jackpot is displayed. The bet wins if the player is dealt a royal flush, a straight flush, four of a kind, a full house or a flush. A hand of a royal flush wins the total jackpot. A straight flush wins 10 per cent of the payout. The payout odds for the additional bets vary from casino to casino. Although the payout odds for the additional bet may seem high, if you compare them to the chances of making the hand you will see that they are poor.

PAYOUT ODDS FOR A PROGRESSIVE JACKPOT

Royal flush 100%
Straight flush 10%
Four of a kind $150–$500
Full house $100–$250
Flush $50–$100

HOUSE ADVANTAGE

Caribbean stud poker has a house advantage of 5.22 per cent. This is slightly more than the other games of poker (5 per cent). The progressive jackpot has a house advantage that is often more than 25 per cent so it is simply not worth playing.

1 Players **A** and **B** each make a bet of one chip in the ante box.
Player **C** makes a bet of two chips.
Five cards are dealt to each player and five to the dealer.
The dealer's last card is dealt face up. It is a 5.
The players look at their cards. Player **A** has 2 pairs.
Player **B** has nothing. Player **C** has a full house.

2 The players now have to decide whether to play or surrender.
Player **B** surrenders and his cards are removed.
The stake (ante) is lost and is removed by the dealer.

❸ Player **A** makes a raise (bonus) bet of two chips (double the value of the original ante bet).
Player **C** makes a raise bet of four chips (double the ante bet of two chips).

❹ The dealer's cards are revealed.
The dealer has three of a kind.

5 The players' hands are revealed in turn.
Player **A** loses both the ante bet and the bonus bet, as the dealer's three of a kind ranks higher than his two pairs.

6 Player **C** has a full house. He wins as his hand ranks higher than the dealer's. The ante bet is paid at evens and the bonus bet is paid at odds of 7 to 1.

Player C holds: J♦   J♥   5♠   5♦   5♣
Dealer holds: 6♠   6♦   6♥   Q♠   5♥

VIDEO POKER

Video poker is a slot game similar to Five-card draw. Much like poker, players can use their knowledge of the game to win. The aim is to win money by making the highest possible ranking hand. The machine incorporates a computer display that shows the player's hand.

The payouts for the various hands are marked on the machine. The highest-ranking hands pay the greatest odds. These payouts vary depending on the casino and the country in which the game is played. Some machines have progressive jackpots. As the game is played, so the jackpot consequently increases.

There are a number of differences from traditional five-card draw. Video poker is played at a much faster pace. It is not always necessary to beat other players' hands. You simply have to get as high a hand as possible. Instead of competing for a pot, you are paid the odds marked on the machine. In addition, no bluffing is involved.

There are several versions of the video poker game. The most popular games available are Jacks or Better, Deuces Wild and Joker Wild. The easiest and most entertaining game to play is Jacks or Better.

HOW TO PLAY

▶ The aim of video poker is to make the highest possible ranking hand on the machine's payout schedule. The minimum hand needed to win varies with different games.

▶ Enough coins need to be inserted into the machine to play, so an ample supply of them need to be kept on hand. The required amount will be marked. Often the stakes are in multiples of five coins. When you press the 'deal' button, the cards will be dealt. A five-card hand will be displayed on the screen. The player has the choice of either keeping the hand or improving it with new cards. If a winning hand is dealt, the machine will either beep or a light will flash. Winnings are paid out.

▶ If a player does not initially have a winning hand, he can select the cards to be kept and decide on those to be discarded. The cards are kept by pressing the 'hold' button corresponding to that card. Once the selection has been made, the player needs to press the 'deal/draw' button for the discarded cards to be replaced. The machine will subsequently deal the new cards. If the hand wins, the winnings are paid out.

The ranking of hands

The hands are ranked in the same way as five-card draw (see p108). Some games allow wild cards to be played. The addition of wild cards gives an extra hand of five of a kind. The payout odds for this hand are marked on the machine. A royal flush made with a wild card is often treated as a lower ranking hand compared to a regular royal flush.

PAYOUT ODDS FOR DIFFERENT GAMES

The odds given below are intended as a guide and will vary depending on where the game is played.

DEUCES WILD

Deuces Wild incorporates the 2 cards as wild cards. A 2 can be used to represent any card. For example, a hand of two kings, two jacks and a two will represent a full house of three kings and two jacks, where the two replaces a king. In most instances, the use of wild cards makes it relatively easier to get a higher ranking hand. The minimum winning hand is three of a kind.

PAYOUT ODDS

Hand	Payout per coin
Royal flush	varies
Four deuces	200
Royal flush with deuces	25
Five of a kind	15
Straight flush	9
Four of a kind	5
Full house	3
Flush	2
Straight	2
Three of a kind	1

JACKS OR BETTER

Jacks or Better is the most popular game. The lowest winning hand is a pair of jacks. Minimum stake is five coins.

PAYOUT ODDS	
Hand	**Payout per coin**
Royal flush	250–800 or progressive jackpot
Straight flush	50
Four of a kind	25
Full house	6–9
Flush	5–6
Straight	4
Three of a kind	3
Two pairs	2
Pair of jacks or better	1

Some simple tips for Jacks or Better

Hold any hand of a straight or over. If:
- four cards to a royal flush are held, draw one.
- four cards to a straight flush or a flush are held, draw one.
- three of a kind, draw two.
- two pairs, draw one.
- one pair, draw three.
- three-card royal flush, draw two.
- four-card straight, draw one.
- three-card straight flush, draw two.
- two high cards of either J, Q, K, A, draw three.
- three high cards, hold two of the same suit. If you hold different suits, then hold the two lowest-ranking high cards.

JOKER WILD

Joker Wild is played with 53 cards. The extra card, a joker, is the wild card. The addition of the wild card makes a higher ranking hand much easier to achieve. The minimum winning hand is a two-pair.

Look for machines paying the best odds. Those with a progressive jackpot enable players to win a high jackpot. Select a machine that has already accumulated a large jackpot. A jackpot is usually paid out after 45 hours of fast play. If there is already a large jackpot on the machine it will be possible to win it in a shorter period.

PAYOUT ODDS	
Hand	**Payout per coin**
Royal flush	varies
Five of a kind	100
Royal flush with joker	50
Straight flush	50
Four of a kind	20
Full house	8
Flush	7
Straight	5
Three of a kind	2
Two pairs	1

THE LUCK OF THE DRAW

Winners and Cheats

Winners are hailed as heroes, and gamblers try many different methods to win at casinos. Some players rely on luck or try to devise systems to overcome the house advantage. Others simply cheat. The man who broke the bank at Monte Carlo did so over a century ago but he is still remembered by gamblers who try to emulate his success. Nowadays, with the proliferation of slot machines, more and more giant jackpots are being won; particularly since the innovation of linked machines.

As cheats' methods have become increasingly sophisticated, so too have the casinos' means of detection. Closed-circuit television, plain-clothes security staff and changes to dealing procedures have all been introduced to deter cheats. Suspected culprits are constantly watched, and barred from the casino if caught.

WINNERS

THE MAN WHO BROKE THE BANK AT MONTE CARLO

The most famous roulette player of all time is the man who 'broke the bank' at Monte Carlo, Charles Deville Wells, an Englishman who arrived at the casino in Monaco on 19 July 1891.

With a stake of FF100,000 he played roulette for eleven hours, winning FF250,000. He had similar good fortune on his second day at the casino. On the third day he lost FF50,000 on roulette but recovered his loss by playing a card game called *trente et quarante*, before he returned to roulette and succeeded in breaking the bank a dozen times, winning half a million francs.

Breaking the bank in a casino does not mean that the casino is bankrupt. It simply means that the table has to replenish its float of cash chips before play can continue. At that time, as a publicity stunt in Monte Carlo, the table would be draped in a black cloth if the bank was broken. This ceremony was specially designed to attract enormous attention on the gaming floor. The black cloth would remain on the table whilst the float was replenished. Players would see this and be encouraged to bet more in the hope that they, too, could break the bank some day.

Nowadays it is not at all unusual for the bank to be broken on a table and it can happen several times in one night. The float is simply replenished with chips at the utmost speed so that the process of gaming is not interrupted.

Charles Deville Wells returned to Monte Carlo in November 1891 and continued to win. But in 1892 his luck ran out, and he began to lose heavily. He was eventually arrested in Normandy for trying to sell coal he had stolen from a steam yacht, and extradited to England. He was convicted of fraud for swindling investors and sentenced to eight years in prison. Wells' good luck on the tables was highly publicized and started a gaming boom in Monte Carlo. In 1892 a music hall song written about him became a hit in the UK and USA.

Going for gold

Another Englishman who had success on the roulette tables at Monte Carlo was Joseph Hobson Jaggers, a worker at a textile mill in Bradford. With his experience of the textile industry, he knew that wooden spindles were subject to wear and tear. On a visit to Monte Carlo in 1873, Jaggers was interested in the mechanics of roulette wheels. He realized that if the spindles of the roulette wheels were worn, the wheels would not be perfectly balanced. This would mean that some numbers would come up more often than others. He theorized that if he could find such a wheel, he could develop a system for winning.

Jaggers employed six clerks to record each number spun on the roulette wheels for an entire day's business. He then spent hours analyzing the data that had been collected. After six days he discovered a wheel where nine of the numbers were spun with greater frequency than the others. He began gambling and four days later he had won US$300,000.

The casino retaliated by switching the wheels around after the close of business and the following day he lost heavily. He then realized that a small scratch he'd noticed on the winning wheel was missing. Searching through the casino he rediscovered his lucky wheel and resumed play, winning US$450,000.

The casino then changed the design of the wheels. The fret (metal strip) that separates the numbers was made movable. Each night the operators put the fret in a different position. Jaggers started losing and decided to quit gambling, retiring with a profit of US$325,000 – the equivalent of more than $3 million today.

In 1880 Monte Carlo was the venue for another coup on the roulette tables. This time a team of 18 Italians operated in shifts, playing for 12 hours a day over a period of two months. Their efforts paid off with a win of US$160,000.

ALBERT HIBBS AND ROY WALFORD

In 1947 Chicago graduates Albert Hibbs and Roy Walford took a motorcycle trip to Reno, Nevada. After studying the frequency of the numbers spun on the roulette wheel at the Palace Club, they determined that number nine was a particularly good bet. With a stake of $100 the pair started playing roulette. After 40 hours they had won $5000. The Palace retaliated by switching the wheel but, confident they had a winning system, they went on to another club, Harolds. Using the same method they increased their win to $14,500. Then they started to lose heavily and with just $6500 left decided it was time to quit.

Their success gained them so much publicity that when they went to the Pioneer Club in Las Vegas a year later, a casino manager recognized them. As a publicity stunt, he staked them $500 and invited them to try their luck at roulette. Hibbs and Walford put their system into action. After one month's play they had won $33,000 but their winning streak was brought to an abrupt end when the owner politely asked them to leave.

In 1986 Billy Walters challenged the Golden Nugget in Atlantic City to a 'freeze-out' game of roulette.

The terms he proposed were that he would deposit $2 million at the cash point, which the casino was required to match. Walters said he would play until either he had won the casino's $2 million or they had won his. Management agreed and play commenced. With each spin of the wheel, Walters played bets of $2000 on five numbers. He won the casino's $2 million stake. He then asked if the casino wanted to continue playing. Expecting to get its money back, management agreed. Walters won $3.8 million.

LEFT *At night, The Strip blazes with colour, as neon lights up the desert skies of Las Vegas and rich and poor alike come out to stake their claim to a slice of the gambling cake.*

RIGHT *In 1947 Albert Hibbs and Roy Walford used perseverance and a simple betting system to win significant amounts at roulette.*

Successful roulette players

In 1958 two students from Nevada, known as the Jones boys, played eight neighbouring numbers on one roulette wheel for 40 hours and won $20,000. Their winning streak was cut short by the casino management who promptly barred them.

In Argentina, two teams of players, headed by Artemeo Delgado and Helmut Berlin, won over US$1 million on roulette over a period of four years.

After Dr Richard Jarecki was barred from the casino in Monte Carlo for excessive wins, he tried his luck at San Remo in Italy. His journey paid off when he won more than US$1 million from playing roulette. In 1981 it took a team of players headed by Pierre Basieux just five months to win over $150,000 in Monte Carlo.

BELOW *Monte Carlo Casino, where the all-time famous roulette player, Charles Deville Wells, won FF250,000 in 1891.*

THE WORLD'S BIGGEST SLOT MACHINE JACKPOT

Slot machines are always popular because they pay out potentially huge jackpots for small stakes. A 25-year-old Los Angeles software engineer won the world's biggest slot machine jackpot in March 2003 at the Excalibur Hotel and Casino in Las Vegas (see p47). After making bets totalling $100 on the $1 Nevada Megabucks slot machine he won $39,713.

The Nevada Megabucks slot machines are located in 157 Nevada casinos. Each time any of these machines is played, the jackpot increases until it is eventually won.

TOP *Progressive jackpots, linked to slot machines, hold the promise of big wins for persistent players.*

Using computers to win

Casinos ban players from using computers, as they can help players quickly spot a pattern on roulette or keep track of cards dealt at blackjack, making it easier to win.

In 1977, a US team led by Ken Uston developed a computer that could be built into shoes and programmed to help players win at blackjack. Data was fed in by using the toes to manipulate buttons, and information relayed back by spikes which touched different parts of the feet. The shoe computers netted the team more than $100,000 at an Atlantic City casino. One of the computers was confiscated by the FBI who concluded the team had not cheated, as the computer had merely processed public information.

CHEATS

Cheating is as old as gambling itself. Archaeological digs of Roman relics have turned up dice made from various materials including ivory, gold, silver and gemstones, but loaded dice have also been found. Dice are loaded by incorporating weights on one side to make them land more frequently on desired numbers.

Cheating seldom is worth the trouble or the risk of being caught, especially not for some 19th-century professional gamblers who made their living on the Mississippi riverboats. Their profits came more from cheating than from fair play. In the early 1800s there was a backlash against card sharps as it was generally believed that they ruined the economy, committed crimes and debased the morality of society. An example of this was in 1835 in response to a drunken gambler who ruined the July 4 celebrations in Vicksburg Mississippi: a vigilante group ran him out of town. Five more gamblers refused to leave and Dr Hugh Bodley, who led a citizen's raid on their gambling den, was shot and killed. The five gamblers were lynched by the mob.

TOP *Cheaters will always find a way to delude their opponents, as depicted by these innovative card sharps in Irving Sinclair's 1944 oil painting* The Poker Game.

THE ART OF DECEPTION

▶ There are many ways to cheat at card games. In poker, knowing your opponents' hands is extremely useful. This is achieved by marking the backs of certain cards in a subtle way so they can be 'read' by the cheat. Methods used include applying a small amount of a chemical that shines or glows, or using a spiked implement to make an indentation in the card.

▶ A skilled card sharp can shuffle the cards in an apparently normal manner but will put them into a specific order to ensure he gets a good hand. Cutting the cards is not a problem. A card with a slight crease down the centre is used to mark the cut and a quick one-handed shuffle puts the cards back into their orig-

inal position. A card sharp can also deal cards from the bottom of the pack or deal the second card from the top, saving the top card for himself.

▶ Values are printed on the corner of cards so cheats need to see just a small piece to know another player's hand. Metallic lighters, glass ashtrays and specially adapted rings containing mirrors are used as reflectors. The cheat positions the object on the table and passes them over the reflector as the cards are dealt.

▶ Cheats also collude with one another. Working in a team they make pre-arranged signals to ensure the player with the best hand stays in the game whilst the others fold.

MODERN-DAY SCAMS REVEALED

In 1999, a blackjack cheating operation was uncovered in South Africa. It was discovered that the printing plates for blackjack cards had been altered so that marked cards were produced. They were unwittingly made by Protea Playing Cards, a company that supplied the local casino with blackjack cards. One of the factory's employees had altered the printing plates so as to produce a mark on the 10s, picture cards and aces. This helped blackjack players win. The marked cards had a small blank space inside a repeated floral pattern on the edge of the card, which was positioned where it could be seen inside the shoe.

The owners of Caesar's Casino in Gauteng became suspicious when their receipts from blackjack fell from 14 to 11 per cent. It is thought that the information on the marked cards was sold to gamblers. It's impossible to say exactly how much was won but a group of four gamblers allegedly won R2 million. The cheats, however, got away with their scam as the gambling laws in South Africa make it very difficult to gain a conviction.

In yet another conspiracy, a former employee of the Nevada Gaming Board of Control, Ronald Dale Harris, used his extensive computer knowledge to modify the programming of slot machines. He was responsible for checking that the slot machines in casinos were fair. This gave him the opportunity to effectively reprogramme the machine's computer chips.

His program was engineered so that if a certain sequence of coins was put into the slot machine, it would automatically pay out the jackpot. With inside knowledge, he also devised a way of using a computer to predict winning plays at keno and video poker. In 1994, he won $10,000 from a Las Vegas keno machine. He was arrested after his accomplice, Reid McNeal, won $100,000 keno jackpot at Bally's Park Place in Atlantic City on 13 January 1995.

Suspicions were raised when McNeal asked to be paid in cash and produced a driver's licence with a different address to the one given when he had checked into his hotel. Investigators went to his hotel room and found Harris there. In January 1998 he was subsequently sentenced to serve seven years in prison.

More recently in England, Reset Ertas and Mesut Yil from Istanbul, Turkey, were caught cheating at poker in the Ritz Casino in Piccadilly. Their method was to cause a distraction so that they could swap cards underneath the table. After winning £8000 they left the casino, but returned a few hours later and started playing again. The casino received an anonymous tip about their scam and the police were called. They continued winning another £4400. Just as they were ready to cash in their winnings, they were arrested. In May 2003, the pair was jailed for six months.

RIGHT *The lure of instant riches draws many visitors to Auckland's Sky City.*

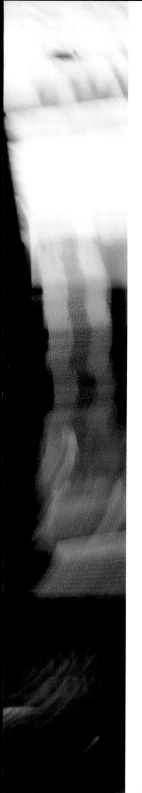

A Few Words
of Advice

Gaming is all about winning and losing, so it makes sense to manage your money effectively. It is easy to get carried away by the excitement, and lose your stake. By understanding the rules of the game, the odds paid, the chances of winning, and when to quit, players can ensure a pleasant casino experience. Gambling should be treated like any other form of entertainment. Expect to spend your money and have a good time doing so. Unfortunately gamblers not only want to win, they actually expect to win and can take it extremely badly when they lose. Even professional gamblers can delude themselves into thinking they either always win or break even.

▶ Take care of your chips and money, and beware of criminals who use the distraction of the games to pick pockets and snatch chips.

▶ Only exchange chips or money with casino staff. There may be a queue at the cash point but at least you will be sure you are not being passed counterfeit money or chips. Ask for big wins to be paid by cheque (check).

▶ Only bet money you can afford to lose. If you gamble regularly, set a budget for gambling and stick to it. Limit the amount of cash you take to the casino and leave cheque books, cash cards and credit cards at home if you think you will be tempted to use them.

▶ Many casinos have cash machines (ATMs) on the gaming floor, making it easy to obtain money. Avoid credit facilities. If you haven't got it, don't spend it!

▶ Rules of play may differ in various countries, so be sure you understand the rules where you are playing. If you need anything explained, speak to a casino manager – do not rely on the advice of other players.

▶ Understand the odds and compare the true odds of each game to the odds paid by the casino. Some games offer better value than others. Each game has a variety of bets, often with different house advantages. On some bets this is so high the bet is not worth playing. Find out the house advantages for individual bets before you begin playing.

▶ Although many games rely on luck, in blackjack and poker, the outcome can be largely influenced by skill. If you play card games, practise them regularly at home. Novice poker players are a great source of income for professionals, as an inexperienced player is no match for someone with years of experience.

the next spin. It is usually left to ride for three spins. A bet straight up on a number is capable of winning 105 chips before it is removed. If you do not claim your winnings you will lose them.

▶ Take account of the additional costs involved in visiting a casino. Transport, tips, admission charges or membership fees, refreshments and other non-gaming activities, such as shows, cinemas, shopping and sports facilities, can add up if costs are not monitored.

▶ Check your payouts. Learn how to calculate the winnings on your bets. Due to the speed at which the games are dealt, casinos can make mistakes. Winning bets get missed and payouts are incorrectly calculated. Confusion can arise when chips are worth more than one stake unit. The inspector checks only large payouts. If you disagree with a payout, query it with the inspector. If it becomes necessary, the camera can be checked to verify your claim.

▶ Learn how to play the games by reading the rules provided by most casinos. Most players do not learn the rules until something goes wrong.

▶ Many casinos offer regular lessons to explain the games and it is worth attending these. Watch other players in action. It costs nothing to be a spectator and a lot can be learned from experienced players.

▶ Don't forget that winning bets on roulette are left to ride. Many players leave the table and forget they still have a bet on

TOP LEFT *Casinos are 'one-stop' sources of entertainment, not only offering gambling opportunities but also an array of shows, cinemas, shopping and sports facilities, which should be budgeted for if one is to make the most of such an experience.*

A FEW WORDS OF ADVICE

SUBLIMINAL PRACTICES

▶ Casinos use a variety of subliminal practices to ensure they get the maximum amount of money from their many visitors before they get anywhere near a gaming table.

▶ Casino design is no accident. Almost every architectural feature is built in with profit in mind. Exteriors are lavish and use every marketing trick in the book to get players to walk through the door. This is taken to the extreme in Las Vegas, where shows put on outside the casinos get people to stop and watch, and, hopefully, entice them to go inside.

▶ Many resort casinos have adjacent shopping malls. The idea is that one moment you're browsing around a shop, the next you're inside a casino. Some casinos in Las Vegas are connected to neighbouring casinos by monorails and moving pavements (sidewalks).

▶ A casino operator knows that the longer players remain inside the gaming hall, the more money they are likely to spend, so every need of theirs is painstakingly and carefully catered for with this purpose in mind. If you are a hotel guest, a car jockey will offer to park your car, while day visitors are provided with convenient transport from the parking lot to the casino entrance.

▶ Waiters deliver food and drinks directly to the gaming tables. Many casinos supply free alcohol, as they know that a drunken player is less likely to care about losing. As many casinos are situated in hotels, players also have the option of simply sleeping off their hangovers on the premises.

▶ Casinos have gone to great lengths to ensure that players do not get bored, by offering every type of top quality entertainment, from lavish variety shows to live sports events. There is also a full range of sports facilities.

▶ Players' awareness of time is reduced. Casinos do not have clocks and the dealers do not wear watches. In the artificial environment, it is always night-time.

▶ On entering the gaming hall, players encounter the slot machines. The flashing lights, bright colours, high noise levels and the hope of winning a big jackpot are all designed to attract customers. The slot machines are deliberately positioned so that players spend all their loose change on their way into and out of the casino. The slots are the most profitable games for the casino as they pay out on average only 75 to 80 per cent of the total amount staked.

▶ A recent innovation has been the development of an odour that makes players bet more on the slot machines. It was developed by the US-based Smell and Taste Treatment and Research Foundation. In trials carried out in Las Vegas, slots adapted to emit the odour produced a 45 per cent increase in business.

▶ Visitors who just take a look inside a casino out of curiosity might be handed a few gaming chips. As these can only be exchanged at the tables, they are encouraged to place a few bets.

▶ Players' associations with 'real' money can decrease when they exchange their cash for a pile of seemingly worthless plastic chips. An entire stack fits nicely into your hand and it's tempting to put a number of chips on a single bet. Cash chips have a value printed on them but table chips do not, so it is very easy to forget their worth. Smart cards and coinless gaming reduce the link with cash even further.

▶ At first glance, the advertised minimum stake for a casino may seem attractively low. However, casinos normally only have a few low-staking tables or slot machines which are usually very crowded, especially over weekends or holiday periods. To avoid the inconvenience of waiting in long queues for these popular games, budget for slightly higher stakes and enjoy a more relaxed casino experience.

▶ When a player appears to be on a fortunate winning streak, a technique called 'stepping up' is employed by the casino dealer, who will make up payouts with chips of a slightly higher denomination. If the player continues to win, the value of the chips will be increased again. This is to subtly tempt the player to bet with the higher value chips. By betting higher stakes, players will lose their winnings more quickly.

▶ Casinos hire attractive, friendly personnel. Players wandering undecidedly around the gaming hall may pass an empty roulette table. The dealer will smile in welcome and spin the wheel. Out of curiosity most players stop and watch to see where the ball will land. With a captive audience the dealer will quickly spin again. The spectators will soon be tempted to play.

▶ Table games are played at a fast and furious pace, which gives players little time to think and reappraise their betting position. There is hardly any time between games to count your chips. On roulette, for example, there is an average of one spin a minute. Experienced players know that you don't have to bet each time, but novices often rush to place new bets, particularly if they have won on the last round.

TIPPING

Policies vary depending on local legislation. UK law prohibits the tipping of gaming staff but non-gaming staff (such as waiters or car valets) may receive tips. In the USA it is normal to tip just about everyone. The amount you give is entirely discretionary. At the gaming tables it is usual to give the dealer a tip when you cash in your chips. In Europe, where tips make up a large part of their earnings, the dealers are quite blunt and will remind players not to forget them.

DECIDING WHEN TO QUIT

It may be a good idea to keep a notebook to record your gambling and to help you judge how well you are playing. It is very easy to delude yourself into thinking that you do not lose. If your records reveal that you are losing too much, then you can analyze what is going wrong and take measures to reduce your losses. Maybe you need more practice or you need to modify your betting strategy.

In the USA you will find the record useful if you have a big win, as gambling wins are subject to hefty taxes. Players can offset gambling losses against winnings, but the IRS requires players to keep an accurate record of dates, bets made, address of gaming establishment, names of people with you and the amount won or lost. Complimentaries also count as winnings. In addition, proof of expenditure, like casino receipts and bank records, will need to be shown if you are audited.

PROBLEM GAMING

'Quit while you're ahead' is an old saying that makes sense in most gaming circles. As soon as a winning streak stops, make a conscious effort to stop playing, and take your chips to the cash point and leave. It is easy to fall into the trap of having one last bet, until you run out of chips and your big win has disappeared.

One strategy is to just bet with your original stake money and go home when it is used up. Any winnings are cashed in and saved for the next time.

ABOVE *As a precaution, do not gamble online as the games' high house advantages make it all too easy to lose your high stakes.*

Most people are able to enjoy gambling without it becoming a problem in their lives, but for a small number of people it can become addictive. No matter how hard they try, they may not be able to break the cycle and regain control of their gambling. The first step toward solving addictive or compulsive gambling is to recognize that there is a problem.

SOME SIGNS ARE:

- you view gambling as a way of earning money
- you gamble with money that is intended for living expenses such as rent, food or transport
- you continually exceed your budget
- you need to borrow because you have gambled too much and then end up gambling even more to try to pay back the loans
- all your free time is spent gambling
- you neglect family, friends and work in order to concentrate on gambling.

There are many international and local support organizations, such as Gamblers Anonymous, who are there to offer help. If you feel your gambling is getting out of hand, contact one of them before it is too late. Most have toll-free lines that enable you to speak to a trained counsellor over the phone. Many hold regular meetings where compulsive gamblers can discuss their problems and find solutions. There are also organizations that support the families of gamblers.

Most casinos support responsible gambling as they understand the importance of promoting gaming as an integral part of the worldwide entertainment and leisure industry. Many have established their own counselling services; they assist state or national responsible gaming programmes and support organizations with funding and by handing out brochures or putting up posters advertising their services. Your doctor or health-care provider may also be able to offer advice on counselling services in your area.

Problem gaming can affect anyone, regardless of age, race, gender or social status. As with other forms of addiction, there is no way of telling in advance who might develop problems with gambling. However, the key to rehabilitation and recovery is early detection and intervention, followed by the appropriate form of treatment. Care and support by professionals as well as friends and family, are the first steps to recovery.

Gaming should be fun – just remember to gamble with your head and not with your heart.

A replica of the Sphinx stands guard over the world's fourth largest pyramid at the Luxor, a renowned casino and hotel complex, in Las Vegas. The interior walls are slanted, and the escalators move at a 39° angle.

GAME SPEAK

BACCARA

Banker The casino.

Prime right The player who is sitting to the immediate right of the banker.

BACCARAT

Banco Banker.

Community cards The same hand that all the players bet on.

Natural A score of 8 or 9.

Ponte/Punto The player.

BLACKJACK

Anchor box The player who is dealt cards first is sitting on the anchor box (see also First base).

Basic strategy A strategy of playing that reduces the house advantage.

Blackjack Traditionally a score of 21 made with an ace and either the jack of spades or clubs (now more commonly an ace and any card worth 10).

Break A score over 21.

Burnt cards Cards discarded by the dealer without being seen by the players.

Bust To achieve a score over 21.

Card counting An advanced technique for reducing the house advantage.

Cut card A blank card used for cutting the deck, used as an indicator of when the cards must be reshuffled.

Double Doubling a bet by increasing it to twice an initial stake.

Draw To take another card.

First base The player who is dealt a hand of cards first.

Hard hand A score of 12 or more.

Heads up Playing alone at a table.

Hit To take another card.

Hole card The dealer's face-down card.

Insurance A side bet that the dealer has a natural. Insurance is offered only when the dealer's up-card is an ace. Players can win double their stake if the dealer has a natural, but lose if the dealer does not.

Natural A hand that scores 21 with the first two cards dealt.

Pontoon Also known as 21; card game on which blackjack is based.

Shoe The box where a dealer's cards are placed (also called *sabot*).

Soft hand A score of 11 or less, meaning a card can be drawn without busting.

Stand To take no more cards.

Stand off A tie with the dealer.

Stiff hand A score of 12–16.

Surrender To give up half your bet for the privilege of not playing out a hand. (In roulette, you effectively lose only half on an even-money bet when the ball lands on 0.)

Third base The spot nearest the dealer's right hand, which will be played last before the dealer's hand is played.

Up card The dealer's face-up card.

CRAPS

Aces 2 (a pair of 1s).

Ace deuce 3.

Active Bets that are on.

All the spots we got 12.

Atomic craps 12.

Boxcars 12.

Boxman Inspector.

Come out First roll of the dice.

Craps A score of 2, 3 or 12.

Easy A score that is not a hardway, for example, a 6 made with 4 and 2.

Front line Pass and come.

Hardway The same score on both dice.

Hopping The roll betting.

Inactive Bets that are off.

Little Joe (from Kokomo) 4.

Miss out Losing score.

Natural Score of 7 or 11 on the first roll.

Ninety days 9.

Ocean liner 9.

On the hop A one-roll bet.

Press To increase bets.

Prop bets Proposition bets (craps bets and hardways).

Push the bet A tie (that is, it is not lost).

Seven out A score of 7 made after the come out roll.

Six five no jive 11.

Shooter The person who throws the dice.

Stickman The dealer who moves the dice.

Square pair 8 (pair of 4s).

Up pops the devil 7.

POKER

All-in A player who runs out of funds, but still plays for the portion of the pot to which he has contributed.

Ante A small portion of the minimum bet that each player is required to put into the pot before a new hand starts.

Big blind When a player who is sitting behind the dealer in Texas hold 'em makes a second bet that is double the value of the first bet made.

Bluff To pretend you have a good hand.

Board The community cards dealt face-up in the centre of the table are referred to as being on the 'board'.

Bring-in In seven-card stud, a mandatory bet made, by the player with the lowest up-card, in the first round of betting.

Dead man's hand A pair of aces over eights, so dubbed when James Butler 'Wild Bill' Hickok, lost his life in a poker game due to this hand.

Draw button It allows the player in video poker to draw up to five new cards.

Family pot When all the players at the table decide to contribute to the pot.

Fifth street In seven-card stud, the third round of betting is called 'Fifth street' because players have five cards. In Texas hold 'em, 'Fifth street' is the fifth card on the board.

Flop When three of the community cards are dealt face up in the very first round of betting in Texas hold 'em.

Flush Five cards of the same suit arranged in any numerical order.

Fold To withdraw from the game and lose all the money you have staked.

Forced bet The bet made by one player to get the betting started.

Fourth street In seven-card stud, the second round of betting is called 'Fourth street' because all of the players have four cards. In Texas hold 'em, 'Fourth street' denotes the fourth card, and the third round of betting.

Full house A hand consisting of three of a kind and a pair.

High poker Standard poker, as compared to low poker or lowball. In high poker, high hands win.

Highest card The card in a hand that determines a winner.

Inside straight Four cards of a straight where the straight can only be completed one way.

Kicker In a draw poker game, an odd high card that doesn't contribute to a straight or a flush; usually an ace or a king.

Limit Any game that has a fixed limit on how much each player can bet or raise in each round.

Low poker Also called lowball, is poker in which the pot is awarded to the hand with the lowest poker value.

Muck pile Where losing cards are placed.

Nuts The best possible hand in Omaha.

Open The player who bets first.

Pat In draw poker, a hand that does not need any more cards. (In blackjack, this would denote an unbusted hand that is worth at least 17 points.)

Pot The total stakes played for in poker.

Qualifier The minimum standard a hand must meet in order for it to be eligible for part of the pot.

Raise When a player raises a previous bet and then bets more, to increase the stake for remaining players.

Rake The money that the casino charges for each hand of poker. This is usually a percentage (five to 10 per cent), or a flat fee that is taken from the pot after each round of betting.

River The final card dealt in seven-card stud or Texas hold 'em. In seven-card stud, staying in until the final round of betting is called 'going to the river'.

Royal flush An ace-high straight flush, the best possible hand.

GLOSSARY

Action The amount of money wagered. In poker, the placing of money into a pot.

Active player Any player who is still contributing to the pot.

Bank Roll Total sum of money a player is willing to risk at the casino.

Banker In a card game, either the dealer, or the players, who book the action of the other bettors at the table.

Bet The maximum amount allowed to be wagered in any game.

Betting limits In a table game, the minimum and maximum amounts players can wager on one bet. They cannot wager less than the minimum or more than the maximum amount posted.

Black The most common colour used for $100 chips.

Blind bet A bet that certain poker players are required to make because of their betting positions.

Break-even point The point at which, if you played indefinitely, the bets you made would approximately equal the payoffs you'd receive.

Buck A $100 wager.

Bug A joker.

Bump To raise.

Burn card After a shuffle and cut, one card is placed on the bottom of the deck or in the discard tray. This is called burning the card.

Cage The cash point on the gaming floor.

Call To bet the same as a previous bet.

Card counting Keeping track of all cards placed since their shuffle.

Card sharp An expert at cards.

Car jockey The person employed to park customers' cars.

Carousel A circle of slot machines with a change person in the centre.

Cash chips Casino currency used to buy into games, place bets, pay for food and drinks and tip staff.

Cashier's cage Where players redeem their casino chips for cash. (See Cage).

Casino rate A reduced hotel-room rate that casinos offer loyal customers.

Chips Tokens used on casino gambling tables in lieu of cash.

Check Another term for a chip. (In poker, a player can 'check' in order to stay in the game but not bet.)

Chip tray A tray, in front of a dealer, that holds that table's inventory of chips.

Cold A player who is on a losing streak, or a slot machine that isn't paying out any winnings.

Cold deck A deck of cards arranged in a specific order.

Colour Table chips for roulette.

Colour up When a player stops betting and exchanges smaller-denomination chips for larger ones.

Comp An abbreviated term that is used to describe the complimentary benefits a casino offers its favoured players.

Court cards King, queen, jack.

Credit button The button, in slot or video machines, that allows players to bank coins in the form of credits.

Cut When a dealer divides a deck into two parts and inverts these after they have been well shuffled.

Cut card A blank card used for cutting a deck of cards.

Deal To hand out cards during a hand.

Dealer Casino employee who deals cards.

Deuce A two.

Die Singular for dice.

Dime bet A $1000 wager.

Dollar bet A $100 wager.

Double down Placing an additional wager, up to the amount of the original, on the first two cards of a hand (the player is only allowed one card).

Discard tray A tray on the dealer's right side that holds all the cards that have been played or discarded.

Draw To take another card (to hit).

Drop box A hidden box on the gaming table where the dealer puts money received for bets or chips.

Edge The profit a casino stands to make on all bets made. It is usually expressed as a percentage and is also known as the house advantage.

Even money A bet that pays players back the same amount they wagered, plus their original wager. Shown as a ratio of 1:1.

Expected win rate A percentage of the total amount of money wagered that players can expect to win or lose over time.

Face cards Any jack, queen, or king in a deck of cards.

Flat top A slot machine whose jackpot is always a fixed amount.

Front money The cash or bank cheques that are deposited with the casino to establish credit for a player who then bets against that money.

Fouled hand A losing hand.

Four of a kind Four cards of the same rank, also known as quads.

Green The most common colour used for $25 chips.

Hand Refers to the cards that players hold, or to the procedure in a card game.

Holding your own Breaking even.

Hot A player who is on a winning streak, or a slot machine that is paying out.

House edge The percentage of each bet players have made that is taken by the house (casino). Winning bets are paid at less than the true odds to generate income for the casino.

Inside bets A roulette bet placed on any number, or small combination of numbers.

Jackpot A big win on a slot machine.

Joker The 53rd card in a deck, sometimes used as a wild card.

Load up To play the maximum number of coins per spin that a slot or video game machine will accept.

Loose Slot machines are loose when they are paying out and giving the house only a small advantage over the player.

Marker A cheque that can be written at the gaming tables by a player who has established credit with the casino

Mini baccarat The scaled-down version of baccarat, played with fewer players, dealers and formality, but following the same rules as baccarat.

Nut Either the overhead costs of running a casino, or the fixed amount that a gambler decides to win in a day.

Odds The ratio of probabilities.

Outside bets Bets that are located on the outside part of the roulette betting layout. These stakes involve betting 12 to 18 numbers at one time.

Overlay A good bet where players have an edge over the casino.

Pair Any two cards of the same rank.